Roswell Martin Field

In Sunflower land

Stories of God's own Country

Roswell Martin Field

In Sunflower land

Stories of God's own Country

ISBN/EAN: 9783743308879

Manufactured in Europe, USA, Canada, Australia, Japa

Cover: Foto ©Andreas Hilbeck / pixelio.de

Manufactured and distributed by brebook publishing software (www.brebook.com)

Roswell Martin Field

In Sunflower land

What the Book Contains.

The Old Crank	9
What Broke Up the Literary	29
He Played with Thomas	53
Tubbs of Kansas	67
How the Lord Remembered Curly	81
The Involuntary Marriage	97
Colonel Bollinger	109
The Deaf Ear	125
The Confession of a Crime	143
The Old Major's Story	163
Sweetheart	177
The Political Wanderings of Joseph Macon	193
The Distribution	207
That Awful Miss Boulder	227
The Luck of Silas Scott	247

THE OLD CRANK.

WESTWARD from the Mississippi, between the thirty-sixth and fortieth parallels of latitude, in the very heart of the greatest nation of the earth, lie two empires. Not empires, indeed, in the common significance of man's imperial sway, with the gay gildings and trappings of the court, and the autocratic rule of royalty, but empires of nature, glorious in the results of a few brief years of experiment, more glorious in the incalculable possibilities of development awaiting the homeseeker. Wherever the traveler goes in these great empires, in wagon, boat or railway car, he sees the monarch of the realm, turn where he may. Far to the north and east, on through the south and west, this jolly monarch keeps at the side of the flying train, to the end of his dominions, where the roads begin to lead to the clouds and the cool air rushes down from the mountains. No traveler asks who this jolly monarch is. No man forgets his allegiance to powerful, affluent, smiling old King Corn.

If Corn is king, then Sunflower is the queen, for hand in hand they go over the wide rolling prairies in their dress of golden yellow, the one typifying

the spirit of industry, the other content with its
lofty bearing and its regal beauty. A worthy
queen is the stately Sunflower to old King Corn.

And, in the main, very happy and contented are
the favored subjects of this prosperous monarch.
For twenty-five, fifty and seventy years of experience have shown them that he is steady and reliable, faithful to those who call upon him, and
never failing those who cultivate him. So these
subjects, with such deviation as national and
political exigency has prescribed, have gone their
ways, content with present abundance and careless
of outside comment; have lived their lives in their
own manner, sung their songs, and cherished their
traditions until modern progress came to the fair
dominion and knocked at the gate. That was the
beginning of the new Missouri and the new
Kansas. Whether it destroyed the charm of the
older life, or by its benefits atoned for the invasion, they may say who will. But is it not true
that the literature, the poetry, the romance of a
country turns to humanity in its simple, original
type, and finds its material where the rushing
spirit of the century has produced the least efface-
ment?

A man who has traveled much through this
land of King Corn, and whose business has brought
him into close contact with the inner life of the
people, once waggishly remarked that Missouri

and Kansas are inhabited by two classes of human beings, Missourians and Kansans. It might have been replied, with Horatio, that "there needs no ghost come from the grave to tell us this," but the jocose gentleman spoke with a deeper significance than the mere words might convey. The fact that underlies the statement, and the fact that impressed itself upon him, is that the Missourian and the Kansan, each in his way, have far more than the ordinary amount of State pride. The Missourian is unaggressive, quiet, but not a whit less proud than the Kansan. He knows perfectly well the ridicule that has been heaped upon his State. He has heard all the songs, all the railroad and circus jokes at the expense of the "Pikers," and, for that matter, he repeats them with a good deal of relish. For he realizes the remarkable resources of his State, its rank in the Union, its illimitable possibilities, its steady and sure growth, and its exemption from the afflictions that have disturbed other less favored commonwealths. He knows that the "Piker" is rapidly passing away, and that, in a few years, "Joe Bowers" will be a myth, and his descendants will repudiate him. Perhaps, even now, the Missourian, as he shrugs his shoulders at the last joke perpetrated by the untraveled Eastern man, thinks to himself that the two jocular bears on the State seal might be credited with the appropriate remark, "He laughs best who laughs last."

The Kansan is a natural fighter. His State had its baptism in blood, and its children have grown up in the atmosphere of battle. It is true of humanity that we always think the most of those things that have cost us the greatest trouble. It is possible that a tendency to exaggeration springs from this same cause. The old-time Kansan is attached to the State he fought for and bled for. There is sincerity even in his exaggeration, and drought, hot winds and grasshoppers, one after the other, cannot silence his tongue or shake his conviction that he lives in God's own country and in the particular locality that the Creator would select for his terrestrial residence. No reasoning, no logic can confound the Kansan. Figuratively speaking, you may knock him down, but you cannot knock him out. As an instance in point, it is related that one day, after a seemingly endless stretch of the most horrible weather, the sun came out. The air was soft and balmy, the sky took on the deep summer blue, and all the conditions were as perfect as the most exacting could demand. The Kansas man was equal to the occasion, and began to descant on the beauties of the Kansas climate. "Now, this," he said, "is a typical Kansas day."

"But how about yesterday, and the day before,

and the day before that, and last week, and the week before?" asked the stranger within the gates.

"Oh," answered the Kansan, perfectly unabashed, "that is the kind of —— weather we used to have back in Indiana."

What can be said to an exuberance, a loyalty and a confidence like that? Why can the world wonder that a State peopled by such enthusiasts, and advertised with such devotion and pride, has grown beyond the limit of precedent.

Every school history of the present day tells under what stormy and peculiar conditions Kansas began to shape itself forty years ago. From the outset it was a Mecca for the eccentric people now commonly known as cranks, and from that day to this not an ism has presented itself to the sisterhood of States that Kansas has not felt its full force. How far these strange people have left their impress on the State, and to what extent they have bequeathed to their descendants an inheritance of whims and fads and fleeting popular fancies, let those answer who can. This tale has only to do with the result of a certain chain of circumstances, the product of peculiar conditions. Depend upon it the hero will stand on his record and consent to be judged at the final day by his merits.

The people who knew him, and had looked him over in all his important bearings and ramifications, agreed that he was just a plain, old-fashioned, every-day Kansas crank.

From this it must not be inferred that everybody who happens to live in Kansas is a crank, and it is not to be contended that everybody who happens to be a crank lives in Kansas. In fact, it is not altogether assured that the Kansas crank is more dangerous or uncomfortable that the Massachusetts crank, or the Mississippi crank, the crank who infests the prairies of Illinois, or the crank who lives in the sage-brush and alkali regions of Nevada. There may be more of him, his ideas may be a little more generally distributed, and he may be more interesting as a panorama of eccentricities, but doubtless he is a very lovable and amusing person, is this Kansas crank, when you do not chance to rub up against his pet theories and regulations of life.

It does not follow that the old Kansas crank was born a crank. In all probability he passed a moderately happy and uneventful childhood in Ohio or Indiana, and came to Kansas in the fifties — suppose we say '57. Those were wild times on the border, and it is worth the trouble and the money to entice an old crank across the prohibition line, and fill him full of good red liquor to loosen his tongue, that he may "shoulder his crutch" and talk about the past: how he "fit with old John," and how many Democrats he sent to the judgment bar. All these things are peculiar to the old crank, but they concern us not at this particular point.

When the war broke out the crank started to the front. He was not much of a crank in 1861, but he was a Union man and a fighter from the top of his bristling hair to the soles of his heavy boots, and the crankier he became the harder he fought, which may be explained on the simple principles of indigestion. He was not one of your sixty or ninety-day fighters. He enlisted for the war, took in every important skirmish that came his way, and went with Sherman to the sea. There is a story to the effect that when he reached the sea the old crank was consumed with regret, and would fain have marched the entire distance back on the same gentle and philanthropic mission.

At the close of the war he returned to Kansas, and, incident to a peaceful agricultural life, was elected to the legislature on an anti-monopoly platform. No man — that is, no Kansan — can be said to have achieved a modicum of worldly distinction and delight until he has been elected to the legislature. The crank was true to his principles: he was chosen as an anti-monopolist, and he walked to Topeka. That was the discharge of the first public duty of the crank.

One day the crank was in Emporia. He was getting along in years, and his lot was lonely.

Political honor had not crowded upon him, and he yearned, or thought he yearned, for the rest and quiet of domestic life. As chance would have it, or, rather, as fate invariably directs it in this modest town of Emporia, he was persuaded to attend a "social" at the State normal school. Now there are various kinds of amusement in this carnal world, but the decision is, from the examination of such data as can be collected, that a "normal social" is, of all diversions, the most unoffending and innocuous. It is related of a certain eminent Methodist divine, who is now with John Wesley in the mansions, that, gazing upon the deep solemnity of one of these "socials," he paraphrased Scripture in saying: "Behold festivities indeed in which there is no guile."

As the crank entered upon the scene of splendor the grand march was in progress, and the happy company, two by two, paraded the hall, singing the Kansas national hymn: "John Brown's body lies a-mould'rin' in the grave." The heart of the crank was stirred. The old war spirit came back, and in the "Glory, glory, hallelujah," he let out his voice with a boom that shook the rafters. And the crank was further attracted by the fine figure of a woman who seemed to be one of the leading spirits of the entertainment. She was, perhaps, thirty years of age, tall, willowy, sharp-featured, with a high forehead, and the unmistakable air of a school-ma'am. Her attire was severely chaste. She was dressed in dove-colored alpaca, high-fitting at the neck, with plain waist and full skirt. Her only ornaments were a pair of mussel-shell ear-rings, and a striking cameo pin at her throat. In her hair, which fell over her temples and curved down and gracefully behind her ears, she had placed a modest wild verbena with shoe-string foliage.

In the opinion of the crank to see her was to love her. To her mind, there never was a more striking illustration of a proper man. Their courtship was brief and fervent. The lady, with the austere simplicity of advanced maidenhood, rehearsed the minute details of her arduous life, and the crank went over and over again the great and irrepressible conflict of the rebellion, wherein he had played a bloody and conspicuous part. And the bride elect looked on her hero with kindling eyes, and, perchance, wished, with Desdemona, that "heaven had made her such a man." And so, in the fall, when the golden tint was on the Kansas forests, they were married, and extended their bridal tour to the State Fair at Topeka, where, hand in hand, they looked at the fat stock, and carefully noted the agricultural products and the latest dairy improvements.

Well, the old crank and his wife went back to the farm, and a pretty middling sort of farm it was.

with its acres of grain, its pleasant orchard and
the little brown frame house near the road. This
house was originally disposed to be whitish, but
the old crank slapped on a coat of brown paint;
something, he said, to be a perpetual reminder of
old John. It was plainly furnished, it is true,
but peace and contentment abode therein, save
when the old crank went on a rural "high,"
which he occasionally did in those unregenerate
days. And the school-ma'am, out of the prompt-
ings of an artistic nature, procured a Hamlin cab-
inet organ, from which, after much internal remon-
strance and apparently piteous protest, she evolved
"The Storm," and "Lincoln's Funeral March,"
and various gems from a collection of war songs,
which besought the boys to "rally 'round the flag"
and to "hang Jeff Davis to a sour apple tree,"
with reminiscences of coming home to die, dear
mother, and of sitting in a prison cell, and of
"marchin' through Georgy." And when the neighbors came in and began to air their accomplishments, the old crank would turn to the good wife
and say: "Marthy, touch us up Gen'ral Persifer
F. Smith's march." And at the conclusion of
this spirited number he would look at the humili-
ated braggarts with a quiet gleam in his eye, as
one who would say: "What do you think o'
that?"

And they had a little library, too. But the old

crank "allowed" he didn't go much on cheap, popular literature, while he could get the Kansas agricultural reports, with an occasional invoice of *Congressional Records*. *Wilder's Annals* lay conspicuously on the table, and a very well-thumbed and dirty page was that which announced the old crank's election to the legislature. And there were also lives of famous Union generals, and the Kansas herd-book, and later on the great campaign record of Blaine and Logan. And there were certain treatises of a spiritual nature from a Wesleyan standpoint, for, as was the custom of the country, the old crank was a stanch Methodist, a class-leader and an exhorter, and, when engaged in fervent spiritual work, his voice could be heard over the bending corn a third of a mile away, heaving wrath and dispensing salvation.

As time went on, the good wife encouraged the old crank to dabble a little in pictures and decorative art. Their first venture was a popular chromo of old Osawatomie. To this was added a stirring picture of General Grant erecting a log cabin. Then followed a framed certificate of life membership in the Bible society; and then, in quick succession, a series of religious scenes and devotional allegories: John Wesley's Death-bed, the three Christian Graces, and Faith clinging to the cross. And one day the good wife brought home "Fruits and Flowers," which she had acquired at an auction, and the gallery was pronounced complete. But in her deft feminine way she went methodically about further to beautify the home; and when the old crank sent out the parlor furniture, tastefully upholstered with horse hair, she worked tidies crocheted in wondrous tints of yellow and green; and one merry Christmas morn the old crank rolled out of bed to stare at "God Bless Our Home" delicately wrought in crewel. Beautiful wax flowers carefully covered with a glass globe rested on a marble-top table, and a dish of luscious wax fruits looked down from the mantel.

To those who gained the full confidence of the old crank he showed his secret treasures, his precious relics of old John. There was the deadly pike with which John Brown went forth to battle for the Lord, and there was the scarf or tippet which he had dropped in a sudden flight. And there were twenty other mementoes, each with its appropriate story. But last, and most precious of all, was a hideous human skull, taken from the loathsome remains of a Platte County Democrat, whom old John had cut off in the flower of his iniquity. And the old crank would roll that skull about in his great horny hands and cry: "His enemies shall lick the dust; his name shall endure forever!"

The old crank was a Granger. It came right along in line with his principles. And very consistent he was, and little found its way into the premises that did not come straight from the Grange store. And he knew a thing about labor-saving machinery, and experimented with windmills and rakes and harrows and pumps and clothes-wringers, and devices for setting hens, and ingenious contrivances for destroying potato-bugs, while little by little they accumulated until they occupied a separate shed. And when the grasshoppers came and made a clean sweep of vegetation, the old crank went out to gaze at the ruin, and he turned and looked at the shed, and said, ruefully: "Marthy, we've got them darned things yet. Even the 'hoppers wouldn't touch 'em."

The Greenback wave swept over the land, and the old crank was the first to send in his allegiance. Mighty were the speeches he made at the local political gatherings, and powerful and irrefutable were his arguments, in the opinion of his admiring neighbors. And in the councils of the Grand Army of the Republic he was the acknowledged chief, and no camp-fire blazed without his presence, and not a pot of beans was cooked that did not feel his practiced touch.

But if there was one subject to which the old crank's soul went unrestrainedly out, it was — pensions. He believed in pensions, for he enjoyed one himself. He had proved beyond cavil that he had lost two-seventeenths of one eye. They gave him

$8 a month. Then he found that he was minus three-eighths of the lobe of a lung. They made it $12. Then he discovered that he was subject to four-elevenths of dysentery. They raised it to $20. Then he stumbled across rheumatism; then his hearing became impaired, the result of the bursting of a shell at Corinth, and at the time of his death he was engaged in proving that he was the victim of chronic catarrh contracted in the Wilderness.

Throughout the State of Kansas there was no more ardent Prohibitionist (in theory) than the old crank. He believed in prohibition because it was "suthin' new and progressive," and because the Democrats didn't believe in it. The old crank hated a Democrat with all the fervor of his strong nature. He hated Missouri because it was governed by the Democratic party. When he went "back east," as he occasionally did, he pulled down the shutters of his window in the car at Kansas City, and neither stirred out nor looked out until the Illinois line was reached. And once, when the train was delayed twelve hours by a wreck, he refused to leave the car to procure refreshment, for, as he subsequently explained to his constituents, he "didn't believe in encouragin' rebel institutions."

Capital punishment was another phase of human industry in which the old crank did not believe.

That is, he did not believe in official executions. But when a couple of frisky fellows made too free with the horses of his immediate neighborhood, the old crank turned out with the boys and hanged them to a cottonwood, explaining that he had every reason to believe "they're Democrats, anyhow." And female suffrage was another of his hobbies. He registered every woman on the place, and on the morning of election he gathered them together and said: "To register and vote is the sacred duty of every man and woman in Kansas, free, glorious Kansas. So we'll now go up and vote for old Bill for mayor." And they did. The old crank saw that they did.

In a national election the old crank's fidelity to the Republican party never waned. Crank though he was, there was no mugwumpishness mixed with his politics. He was red-hot for the nominee every time. When Blaine was nominated the old crank went stark, staring mad. He organized a Blaine club. He went to all the rallies. He made war speeches. He paraded with the boys and spilled coal oil down his back with nightly regularity. In short, he went in to save the country. But when the news came that Blaine was defeated it nearly broke the old crank's heart. "Marthy," he said, "I've seen the 'hoppers come an' nigh eat us out o' house an' home. I've fought the drought an' potato-bugs. I've been down with the malary, an' felt hard times press on us, an' I've never complained. But now I cry out with Job: 'The earth is given into the hand of the wicked; he covereth the faces of the judges thereof. Oh, that I had given up the ghost and no eye had seen me.'"

And on the day of Cleveland's inauguration the old crank dressed up in his blue uniform, and took down his army musket, and went into the parlor, and sat under the picture of old John, and told Martha to call him "when the boys march by on their way to the front." And the good wife hustled the children off to school, and told the neighbors not to mind him, for the old man was getting sort of childish.

Not many weeks thereafter the summons came. The old crank was taken down with bronchitis — true to his principles he called it brown-chitis — serious complications followed, and it was evident that the end was near. It was a glorious June day in Kansas, and a June day in Kansas is one of the glories of this fleeting life. The old crank lay on the bed where he had rested for twenty years. His faithful wife sat by and held his hand, and the pious Methodist parson whispered words of encouragement. A light sparkled in the old crank's eye. Did he catch that glimpse of the celestial beauties which is said to be granted to the departing faithful?

"Is everything bright and beautiful, James?" said the good wife.

"Tol'able," replied the dying Christian, with a faint suggestion of disappointment in his tone, "not as bright as sunny Kansas, but tol'able."

Then the old crank sat up in bed. "I see him, Marthy," he cried, "I see him. I'd know him among a million. It's old John, just as we've seen him in the pictur' in the Historical Society rooms at Topeky, with a halo of glory around his head an' a lot o' little nigger children implorin' his blessin'. He's standin' at the pearly gates, an' seems to be givin' gen'ral directions, sort o' passin' on the papers of candidates. An' I see lots o' Kansans climbin' up the golden stairs, an' imps o' darkness dartin' out to worry an' molest 'em. I know 'em. They're Democrats."

"*Ad astra per aspera*," said the minister, solemnly.

"Amen," replied the weeping wife.

"And I think old John knows me," cried the old crank, exultingly, "for he has said somethin' to the sentry, an' now he smiles an' stretches out his arms, an' the Democrats have fled away. Sing me one o' the old war songs, Marthy, 'Tramp, tramp, tramp.'"

The good wife, her voice broken by her tears, hummed the familiar refrain, and the old crank fell back upon the bed.

"Tell the boys," he whispered, "that I've seen him. I've seen old John. 'His body lies a-mould'rin' in the grave, but his soul goes marchin' on.'"

The old crank's lamp went out.

What Broke Up the Literary.

WHAT BROKE UP THE LITERARY.

No doubt existed in the minds of the community that Pikeville had a good deal to be proud of. For was it not recognized as one of the oldest and most eminently respectable towns in the fine old commonwealth of Missouri, "enjoying," as the mayor said in his welcoming address to a visiting delegation of Boston capitalists, "all the culture and refinement of a long-established Southern aristocracy, quickened and vitalized by Eastern immigration"? Pikeville "pointed with pride" to those splendid old families, the Camdens, the Crawfords, the Dallases, the Lawrences and the Mercers, who, in turn, "viewed with alarm" the inroads of a vulgar "boom," which, however, had left Pikeville the center of a prosperous railway system and with the advantages and improvements of a modern city.

Yet if the question had been put point blank to Pikeville: "On what do you base your hope of greatest renown and well-being?" Pikeville would have risen as one man and replied: "Our Literary."

Now, this "literary" was not a plant of rapid

and immature growth. It was rather the result of a slowly-developed and well-matured decision. It came along partly as the sequence of the boom and the stirring influence of Eastern immigration, and partly through reason of the increased feminine literary activity that was epidemic in the country at large. The immediate cause was the arrival of Miss Sophronia Merrick, of Massachusetts, who had come to Missouri for scholastic missionary work, and had been induced to establish a school in Pikeville, thereunto moved by the charm of the town, the excellence of the water and the courtly hospitality of the people. Miss Merrick was abundantly qualified to lead in literary endeavor, as she had taken a thorough collegiate and post-graduate course; had been an active member of the learned Browning, Goethe, Dante and Ibsen societies of Boston, and could show papers of honorary membership in many of the best organizations for the promotion of human thought. While not a particularly engaging person from a cursory masculine point of view, Miss Sophronia was much esteemed for her mental qualifications, and as she minded her own business, and minded it very well, the generous old families of Pikeville soon came to overlook her unhappy accident of birth in Massachusetts.

Miss Sophronia's intimate friend was Miss Almira Putney, formerly of Vermont. Ezra Putney had moved to Missouri a few years before to go into the fancy stock business, and to exchange a bronchial affection for regular and well-defined touches of malaria. Miss Almira did not possess in the full degree the ripened intellectual charms of Miss Sophronia, but her atmosphere had always been good, and in sundry contributions to the local paper she had manifested an agreeable acquaintance with much that is praiseworthy in literature. Miss Almira had, moreover, not a little of the sturdy independence of the old stock, and in her pursuit of knowledge had imbibed much of the classic and modern thought, which, however conformable to the requirements of a person of wide reading, is not recognized and approved by the Methodist Episcopal Church, to which the greater part of Pikeville owed its allegiance.

The association, then, of two such spirits as Miss Sophronia and Miss Almira could not fail to bring about results most felicitous to the general welfare. Miss Sophronia had looked over the literary condition of the town and had pronounced the trend favorable. She had even delivered a lecture to the ladies on the life, character, writings and influence of Johann Wolfgang von Goethe, preparatory to the formation of a Goethe club; but Miss Sophronia's enthusiasm for the *ewig weibliche* and for ponderous and complex Teutonic philosophy led her into such deep channels that the ladies were soon over their heads. Moreover, Mrs. Dallas confided to the younger ladies that Goethe was a "nasty man," and this idea soon prevailed to the verge of a panic. But the lecture was not altogether a failure, for it stimulated the ladies to the point of doing something. Several meetings were held, and numerous plans discussed. An organization was speedily effected, officers were elected, and a constitution and by-laws adopted. Light refreshments were voted, and, all the preliminaries having been settled, the club took up the question of work.

In view of the inroads made upon previous feminine literary progress in Pikeville by the seduction of progressive euchre, dancing, parties and picnics, to say nothing of the sterner and oft-recurring duties of revivals and protracted meetings, Miss Sophronia and Almira suggested the study of American literature. Posie Mercer, who had just returned from the East, where she had pursued special courses of psychology and china painting, was anxious to take up Tolstoi. Virgie Cooper declared a preference for Ibsen, if he could be obtained in an expurgated and fumigated edition. Sadie Boone, who was thought to be engaged to a young man who traveled for a St. Louis hat house, believed she could give her days and nights to the study of Emerson alone. Winnie Schuyler, fresh from a finishing school, where they called for butter in three languages, spoke for the literature of France; and Mrs. Crawford and Mrs. Dallas, who were sisters, and whose maternal grandfather had lived in Yorkshire, were equally clamorous for an English course, not to ante-date Chaucer, whose spelling and grammar were notoriously poor.

The dispute was settled by a very interesting occurrence. Joanna Brown, whose family had recently come to Pikeville from Kansas, was conversing with Sadie Boone and Daisy Camden when the subject of the Declaration of Independence came up. Miss Daisy chanced to remark casually that the Declaration was promulgated at Guttenberg. Miss Sadie thought Miss Daisy must be mistaken. Miss Daisy was sure she was not mistaken, for she had heard her brother talking about Guttenberg the night before. Miss Sadie was willing to admit that it was something that sounded like Guttenberg, but she thought it was Gettysburg. Miss Joanna was quite positive it was not Gettysburg, as her father had talked about Gettysburg for the past twenty years, and had never mentioned the Declaration of Independence. Just at this point Miss Sophronia, approaching, was horrified. "If this is the extent of your knowledge of your country," she said, severely, "I think we may as well drop all other subjects and take up American history." The girls were too abashed to remonstrate, and the motion was put and carried without an objecting voice.

The decision of the class was most cordially indorsed by the best thought of the community. The editor of the Pikeville *Guard* complimented the ladies in an editorial of unusual felicity of expression, and called them the daughters of Clio, incidentally remarking that no other town in Missouri could present such an aggregation of culture, beauty and true womanliness. To this the Midland *Banner* retorted with cutting sarcasm, which involved both newspapers in a long and acrimonious discussion, from which Pikeville and the *Guard* emerged with added distinction and renewed pride.

In the meantime the class was progressing famously, and so skillful was the leadership of Miss Sophronia, and so helpful the suggestions of her experience, that the young men of the town were in a constant condition of mental depression and becoming sense of inferiority. The essays were not infrequently published in the *Guard*, and although the *Banner*, by the sneaking and reprehensible employment of parallel columns, sought to prove that they were copied literally from encyclopædias and histories, the *Guard* repelled the accusation with such denunciatory vehemence that the society voted the editor thereof a special resolution of thanks, and in turn was honored by the publication of an original complimentary poem, containing many flowers of rhetoric and pearls of thought.

And so matters ran along smoothly. The attendance was large, the ladies were enthusiastic, the tea was delicious, and the beaten biscuits and the macaroons transcended criticism. One day Miss Almira Putney rose to read an essay on the Pilgrim Fathers. As was perfectly natural and commendable, Miss Almira eulogized these gentlemen, long deceased, spoke of their troubles and persecutions, of their strike for freedom of religious conviction, of their heroism, their steadfastness of religious integrity, and of the great impress they left upon the country. When Miss Almira had finished and the matter was before the society for discussion, Miss Daisy Camden observed that while, of course, she could not speak from actual knowledge, she had always understood that the Pilgrims were a common job-lot sort of people. Miss Almira, with rising color, desired to know where she had procured such valuable information. Miss Daisy promptly replied that she had been so informed by her father, Judge Camden; whereupon Miss Almira said "Oh!" with a peculiar and significant intonation. Miss Daisy requested the privilege of informing Almira Putney that her father belonged to the F. F. V.'s, the first families of Virginia. Miss Putney blandly asked permission to enlighten Daisy Camden; that she also belonged to the F. F. V.'s, the first families of Vermont. Miss Daisy laughed a very unnatural and unpleasant laugh, and her dearest friend, Miss Virgie Cooper, tittered. At this point Miss Sophronia interfered, and warned the young ladies that personalities would not be permitted. Miss Daisy explained that personally she had the warmest regard for Almira, and Miss Almira admitted that she was devoted to Daisy. The matter then dropped.

At the next meeting of the society Miss Evie Dallas read a thoughtful essay on the depressing influence of Salem witchcraft. Miss Dallas's parents, as South Carolinians, had transmitted to Miss Evie in natural inheritance a somewhat one-sided view of Puritan character, and the young lady, in the course of literary preparation, interpolated many spicy personal opinions touching the ignorant superstition of the Puritans, particularly exemplified by Cotton Mather.

Miss Tosie Adair was astonished. She could not conceive how anybody could have obtained such opinions of Doctor Mather.

Miss Evie replied that she had consulted her father, the junior member of the firm of Camden & Dallas, and he had told her that Cotton Mather was a crack-brained old fanatic, but that she had decided to mitigate this opinion as unladylike.

Miss Tosie, with blazing eyes, presumed that Miss Evie did not know that she was descended from Doctor Mather through her mother, whose maternal grandmother belonged to the Mathers of Connecticut.

Miss Evie reddened, and said that unfortunately she did not, but since the matter had been brought up she felt compelled to stand by the truths of history.

To this Miss Tosie replied, with a sneer, that since "history" was invoked she would admit that the good people of Salem had been a little hasty; but at least they had acted conscientiously, thinking they were pleasing God, and not from malignance, which had led certain people in other parts of the country to torture and kill poor, unoffending black men.

At this there was a great sensation, and several of the ladies said, "Oh! Oh!" Miss Sophronia called Miss Tosie to order and gently rebuked her.

Miss Tosie apologized to the ladies of the class for anything that might appear unparliamentary, but, as for herself and her family, they did not wish association with anybody who maligned their ancestors. The emphasis on "family" made Miss Evie redden more deeply, and caused the ladies to turn away their heads and smile, for the preference for Miss Tosie's brother exhibited by Miss Evie had been town gossip for months.

When the perplexing and demoralizing subject of the Puritans had been overcome by the happy arrival of the eighteenth century, amicable relations were completely restored. Miss Daisy staid all night with Miss Almira, and Miss Evie, in that deft, winning, woman's way, smoothed things over with Miss Tosie's brother, and declared that a visit to Connecticut was the dream of her life. And so the even current ran along through the French and Indian war, on and past the stirring scenes of the Revolution and the troublous times of 1812. It might be supposed that the various political distinctions of the United States government would have troubled the ladies. Not a bit of it. Each member of the class had her particular essay, and, recognizing the former disasters, the audience always preserved a respectful demeanor, and asked no questions. It was feared that Miss Virgie Cooper's position on the Missouri Compromise might excite a little hostility, but as she refrained from all personal opinions and adhered closely to the text of the authorities, the danger was averted.

In fact the ladies were felicitating themselves that they had now progressed beyond all possible collisions and outbreaks, and were sure of their tempers and good humor. Moreover, such was

Miss Sophronia's tact, and so firm and adroit was her administration, that every tendency toward personalities was quickly repressed. But it chanced that Miss Sophronia was invited to go to Midland to address the young ladies of the Methodist college on the centripetal quality of the Ego, and in her absence the duties of the chair devolved upon the vice-president, Miss Sadie Boone. Miss Sadie entered upon the task with no little trepidation, for, while she was very pretty and popular withal, she knew as little of parliamentary usage as the sacred cow knows about the music of the future.

Unluckily, that day Miss Winnie Schuyler had prepared an essay on the missionary work of John Brown in Kansas. Miss Winnie warmed to her subject, and described the fearful odds against which this heroic man contended in his glorious struggle for freedom. She followed him to Virginia, to Harper's Ferry, and, after he had been executed with due solemnity, she invested him with a martyr's crown and a halo of surpassing brightness.

In the discussion that followed Mrs. Crawford remarked that she supposed that everybody nowadays knew that John Brown was a law-breaker and a thief, and properly suffered a felon's death.

Miss Winnie replied that under the terms of the

Missouri Compromise the extension of slavery had been strictly prohibited.

Miss Daisy Camden thought that the extension of slavery had nothing to do with the case: that John Brown was an old freebooter who pillaged and murdered just for the love of excitement.

Miss Tosie Adair believed that Miss Daisy was unduly influenced by the thought that she must stick up for Virginia.

Miss Daisy emphatically responded that she was not moved by any such consideration; that she merely repeated an opinion which she had heard her father give. And she presumed that the ladies would admit that her father was perfectly competent to give an opinion worth respecting.

Miss Joanna Brown spoke with great agitation and ill-concealed wrath. She gave the ladies to understand that her father had known and fought under Captain Brown in Kansas, and that she had been named in honor of that good man. As a babe she had been held in his arms, and she would allow nobody to asperse his memory while she had a tongue to defend him.

Miss Virgie Cooper jocularly answered that nobody ever doubted that Joanna had a tongue, and Miss Evie Dallas slyly remarked that as John Brown had departed this life thirty years ago, Joanna's remembrance could not be disputed by the ladies present. This keen feminine thrust caused Miss Joanna to wince with pain.

Miss Almira Putney took the floor. She said that in the absence of Miss Sophronia she had endeavored to keep quiet, but that the outcropping of old rebel sentiment was becoming offensive to an unbearable degree. In view of the heated condition of the ladies, she would move an adjournment, but she gave notice that at the next meeting she would throw aside all reserve and produce authorities to place the onus of the civil war on the rebels, where it properly belonged.

In seconding the motion to adjourn, Mrs. Crawford protested against the use of the word "rebels," and promised, on her side, to be present with a counterblast of authorities. And so Miss Sadie Boone, being on the verge of insanity, or at least of tears, declared the meeting adjourned.

When the news of the rupture in the "literary" spread about town, as it quickly did, all Pikeville was in a flutter. Ten years before it would have been impossible to start a discussion of this nature, but immigration had wrought many changes, and Pikeville had even enjoyed the novelty of a Republican mayor. Still the old Southern element strongly prevailed, and in this circle Miss Sophronia was heartily condemned. "Of co'se," said Judge Camden. magnanimously, "the repo'ts that my daughter brings me may be exaggerated, but I reckon the Yankee school-teacher is a mischief-maker." This candid declaration from the Judge was regarded as particularly significant, for his attentions to Miss Sophronia had been noted by all the ladies as presaging a change in his domestic relations.

Miss Sophronia was much distressed by the unfortunate turn of events, and repaired to the Presbyterian minister for advice. The worthy man counseled her to address the throne of grace, but, as she had already done that two or three times without visible results, she despaired of active Providential interference. At last she decided to appeal to the ladies in open session, and trust to their good nature and good sense. In the meantime the most awful condition of affairs prevailed. Miss Tosie Adair had so ingeniously poisoned the mind of her brother that he had broken an engagement to take Miss Evie Dallas to the mite sociable, whereat Miss Evie had spent the night in tears. Miss Daisy Camden cut Miss Almira Putney dead on the street, and Miss Almira, in return, told Miss Daisy's best young man that she now believed that Daisy was descended from Pocahontas because she looked it. Miss Posie Mercer was found to be authority for the story that Miss Winnie Schuyler's grandfather was a common shoemaker in New Hampshire, and Miss Winnie gave it out that a

young man from Boston, who had summered in
Pikeville, had mittened Miss Posie and gone home
in disgust because she spelled "buggy" with one g.
To add to the general perturbation the Midland
Banner came into possession of the facts, and
printed the most atrocious doggerel, satirizing the
ladies, and vulgarly calling upon the young men to
resort to arms, a specimen of low wit which the
editor of the *Guard* promptly and crushingly
rebuked.

When Tuesday afternoon came around, and the
society met at the residence of Mrs. Crawford, the
ladies appeared, their arms loaded with books.
Miss Sophronia saw with uneasiness that the Con-
federates were ranged on one side of the room, and
the Union cohorts on the other. She also noticed
a number of little brothers on the sidewalk, and
gathered from their high juvenile voices and
occasional cries of "Rats" and "Come off," that
preliminary skirmishing had begun. The authorities were piled on the table and sofa. Here was
Redpath's *Life of John Brown*, and here Sheahan's
Life of Douglas. Here Horace Greeley's *Confederate States*, and Alex. Stephens's *War Between the States*, and Jeff Davis's *Rise and Fall
of the Southern Confederacy*, and Pollard's *Lost
Cause*, and Hill's *War on the Border*, and Sneed's
Fight for Missouri, and Johnston's *Narrative of
Military Operations*, and Hord's *War Memories*,

and a dozen other volumes of less note. And last of all came Miss Almira Putney, panting and blowing, and bearing huge books of the *Records of the Rebellion*, looking very wicked and very confident.

Miss Sophronia sighed, and the look of trouble deepened on her countenance. She gave an appealing glance to Miss Almira, who had dropped the *Records* on the carpet with a defiant bang, and cleared her voice and said:

"Ladies, it has been assigned to me to prepare an essay on the causes leading up to the attack on Fort Sumter in our late deplorable civil war. I have not done so, for reasons that will appear perfectly proper to you. The war, ladies, closed twenty-five years ago. I think I may say, without giving offense, that Miss Brown and myself are the only ones present who can recall the slightest phase of that terrible conflict. You, my dear Daisy, were not born, nor you, Virgie, nor you, Sadie, nor you, Winnie, Tosie and Almira. How absurd, then, is it that now in this reunited country we should be governed by the simulation of passions that we have never felt, to the disruption of our pleasant intercourse and the disbandment of our society."

"Almira Putney had no right to call us rebels," said Miss Posie Mercer.

"Excuse me, but I had the right; and here"

(tapping the *Records* significantly) "it is," replied Miss Almira.

"And here," broke in Miss Virgie Cooper, "is Mr. Davis's testimony that you are all wrong."

"Bah!" cried Miss Winnie Schuyler; "how absurd to take the biggest traitor in the pack as an authority on loyalty."

"Winnie Schuyler," said Miss Daisy Camden, passionately, "how dare you call Mr. Davis a traitor? Did you ever see Mr. Davis?"

"No, and I never wanted to."

"Well, I have, and he's no traitor, but a real nice, polite old gentleman. I've got his picture, and his autograph, too."

"Well, you can keep them."

"Thank you, I mean to, and pretty well hidden when there is anybody from Connecticut in the neighborhood."

"If the ladies will remember that they are ladies, and not lose their tempers," said Miss Evie Dallas, with emphasis, "I should like to read a chapter from Pollard's *Lost Cause*."

"Let's see; Pollard was another rebel, wasn't he?" queried Miss Brown.

"No, he wasn't a rebel," retorted Miss Evie, angrily; "he sympathized with the Confederate government."

"With the what kind of government?" asked Miss Brown, tauntingly. "With the Confederate government? Wasn't that the government that supported Quantrell and Anderson?"

"At all events," replied Miss Evie, with tears in her eyes, "it didn't support Red Legs, who came over from Kansas and murdered my uncle John, whom I never saw."

"Well, if you never saw him, what are you crying for?" put in Miss Almira. "I don't believe he ever wasted a thought on his posthumous relations."

"Ladies, ladies!" said Miss Sophronia.

Miss Virgie Cooper rose with great and impressive dignity. "I am not ashamed to say that I am descended from rebels, or whatever you choose to call them, Almira Putney. My grandmother hung a Confederate flag out of her window in the full sight of the Yankee troops, and my father chased a Yankee ten miles into the next county. I am not chasing Yankees myself, but I am not bound to associate with them. Come, Daisy."

Miss Tosie Adair took the floor. "I am going myself," she said, "and Winnie is going with me. I have often heard about plantation manners, and have been anxious for an exhibition. My curiosity is satisfied."

"In handing in my resignation," spoke up Miss Evie Dallas. "I wish to say that I am perfectly shocked by the display of brutality on the part of Northern women. I am glad that my experience begins and ends here."

"So am I," snapped Miss Almira Putney. Miss Almira had a peppery tongue.

One by one the ladies picked up their books, put on their gloves, bowed stiffly to the president and the hostess, and left the room. And then Miss Sophronia, the erudite, the profound, the honorary member of the great Browning, Goethe, Dante and Ibsen societies of the country, the corresponding secretary of the Emersonian Daughters of the Southwest, the founder of the Missouri branch of the Society for the Centripeteney of the Ego, walked over to Mrs. Crawford, put her head on her shoulder, and wept.

The most disastrous results followed the disbandment of the society. Although the *Guard*, ever alert to the interests of Pikeville, carefully excluded all reports of the calamity from its columns, the local feeling was intense, and showed itself in the high social circles. The young man who traveled for a St. Louis hat house was invited by Miss Sadie Boone to thrash Miss Joanna Brown's brother. Having performed this valorous feat, he boasted of it in a billiard room, and was in turn soundly trounced by young Mr. Adair. Hearing of the disgraceful proceeding, Deacon Dallas sent word to young Mr. Adair that as he frequented billiard halls he should come to his house "no mo'." This sentence of proscription sent Miss Evie to her bed for three days. Judge

Camden and ex-Mayor Schuyler came to blows in front of the Methodist church, and the Coopers and the Putneys, who had occupied adjoining pews for five years, declined to mingle as of yore in the consolations of religion.

So things ran on from bad to worse for three months. One evening Judge Camden, whose fifty years sat lightly on him, and who was esteemed the likeliest widower in the country round about, was walking jauntily to the post-office when he encountered Miss Sophronia.

"Good evening, Miss Sophronya," said the Judge, gallantly; "a charming evening."

Miss Sophronia blushed a little, as an elderly maiden should, and admitted that the evening was indeed unexceptionable.

"Miss Sophronya," went on the jurist, "do yo' know, madam, that I feel that in some way yo' and I are responsible for the present strained relations in this community?"

The lady was more agitated than ever. The Judge was a personable gentleman, and in every way qualified to impress a maidenly heart not too young. Moreover, she had been warned to look out for the Judge.

"Feeling, as I said befo', that we are responsible for this state of affairs, what do yo' say, madam, to a sacrifice on yo' part to reconcile the North and the South? Will yo' accept me, madam, as a hostage? Shall it be Virginia and Massachusetts, now and forever, one and inseparable?"

Miss Sophronia was overcome. She did the best thing possible under the circumstances, sat down on a convenient gate step and gasped out: "Why, Judge!"

When it became known that Judge Camden and Miss Sophronia were engaged, all Pikeville weaved and tottered. Miss Daisy flew out to the Putneys, fell on Miss Almira's neck and wept tears of sorrow and joy, and forgiveness, and remorse. Deacon Dallas cordially invited young Mr. Adair to supper, and Miss Evie was at her best. The Putneys and the Coopers occupied the same pew at prayer-meeting, and the representative of the hat firm presented to Mr. Brown one of his very best samples as a token of perfect reconciliation.

"This country," said the Judge, "is all right. What it needs is one or two statesmen to keep things smooth and level, and by mutual concessions to hold the ship of state to its co'se."

But when the Judge stood up in the crowded church, and saw the smiling faces of his old rebel and Yankee friends, and heard the parson's solemn question: "Do you take this woman to be your wedded wife?" he answered:

"I do,"— and with a droll emphasis that set the congregation tittering,— "but no mo' literaries."

4

He Played with Thomas.

HE PLAYED WITH THOMAS.

THE boys had gathered in John Kingman's grocery. It wasn't much of a grocery, but, for that matter, Elk Grove wasn't much of a town; so accounts balanced. Why Elk Grove was called Elk Grove is a question as hard to answer as the fair Juliet's impatient query, "Wherefore art thou Romeo?" Some people ask foolish questions with no expectation of a satisfactory answer. The few houses that composed the town were dumped out on a wide and cheerless prairie in Western Kansas, and, while it is possible that in bygone ages an elk may have passed along on his way to a more congenial stamping-ground, there never was any scientific reason for supposing that a grove could by any chance have been a feature of the place. One argument was that the town originally was Elk Grave, so called from the discovery of bones supposed to belong to the cervine family, and that when the Santa Fé road put up a little station and made out a new time-table a typographical error changed the Grave to Grove, an indignity which the haughty and autocratic magnates refused to rectify. This explanation may be taken for what it is worth, but it is cited merely to show how the railroad power in Kansas has ridden arbitrarily over the intentions and desires of the people.

Evidently the road favored not only offering a slight, but rubbing it in as well, for it persisted in treating Elk Grove as a whistling-station, and trains seldom stopped save to put off a tramp or repair the engine. Indeed, it began to be whispered about that the conductors saved up their tramps for Elk Grove, and it was noticed that when the engineer pulled out he wore a grin hideous in its malignant cunning. Several indignation meetings were called, and it was resolved to carry the matter to Topeka, but the subsequent reflection that the railroad owned the legislature and the entire machinery from Governor down to janitor put an end to that scheme. So the boys soothed their feelings by rallying at John Kingman's grocery and drinking success to prohibition and confusion to tramps and railroad conductors.

On the night sacred to the incidents of this tale the rally was a little larger than usual. The Hanks boys were there, and the Blilers; Bill Cook and his cousin Tom; Sam Chesney, the toughest man in the district; Joe Ardway, with a record of three men; Captain Matthews, the marshal, and two cowboys, visiting the town and always agreeable to anything that promised exercise and relaxation. John Kingman was in good spirits, and as he shoved the dried apples behind the counter and put a few more boards on the cracker boxes, he intimated that the liquor was accessible.

As might have been expected from so sprightly and jovial an assemblage, the conversation turned humorously on the attitude of the railroad toward Elk Grove, and the still more perplexing attitude of the town toward tramps. Joe Ardway contended that Captain Matthews, as town marshal, was derelict in his duty in failing to take extreme measures against the output of through travel. The marshal replied that his duties were circumscribed; that he regretted to say that tramps as a rule had been perfectly peaceable, and that he would not be justified under the statutes and his oath of office in shooting a man whose only offense was breathing.

To this position one of the visiting cow gentlemen, in a perfectly calm and dignified tone, took exception. He pointed out that a tramp without home and money was necessarily a wretched being, whom it would be a kindness to put out of his misery. He believed it was the duty of mankind to alleviate pain and suffering, and he knew of no medicine so quick and sure in action as a bullet administered with a steady hand and an unerring eye.

This opinion excited a general discussion. It

was cordially indorsed by Sam Chesney and the Blilers, and gently criticised by Bill Cook. Mr. Cook believed that it was the sense of the community to breathe a spirit of toleration. He admitted that tramps were no good, and deserved a little touching up, but he couldn't countenance anything worse for a first offense than hanging — not hanging to death, of course, but just long enough to give a good choking and a scare. And he quoted from the beatitudes: "Blessed are the merciful, for they shall obtain mercy." For Mr. Cook was quite a scholar, in his way, and, rumor said, had taught in Sunday-school back east.

The calm judicial manner and scriptural quotation were not without a quieting effect on the audience, already slightly inflamed by the potency of Mr. Kingman's hospitality, and the convention had settled down to the discussion of the minor penalties of mob law, when three sharp whistles signaled the approach of the night express from the west. Bill Cook shrugged his shoulders, the Bliler boys laughed, and Joe Ardway looked significantly at Captain Matthews and grunted:

"Tramps!"

Mr. Kingman was equal to the emergency. He lighted the lantern and passed it to the marshal, who took it and walked out without a word, the boys falling in in single file. When fifty yards from the station, they saw the conductor on the platform raise his foot, give it a careless, easy swing, and a dark object shot from the train and rolled over into the ditch. Somebody called out, "Go ahead;" a sardonic laugh floated back from the cab; the bell rang, and the express puffed off to the east.

The night was dark, and the marshal flashed his lantern vigorously before the dark object was seen wiggling up the sides of the ditch like a copperhead in a cactus. "I've got him," said Sam Chesney. "Come up to the hotel, young feller, and join in the festivities you've interrupted."

So back to the grocery the party went, the shivering tramp surrounded by his captors, who regaled him with fragmentary discourse touching the last public execution in Elk Grove. And when Kingman had lighted another lamp in honor of the occasion, they shoved him into the middle of the room for general examination.

He was not a young fellow after all, but a middle-aged man, the picture of woe and degradation. He was emaciated, ragged and dirty beyond the usual limitations of the tramp. His clothes were marvelous in their infinite variety. Hunger and disease showed in his sunken eyes and cheeks, and he tenderly passed a trembling hand over the contusions produced by his fall and the conductor's boot.

"Well," said Joe Ardway, "what do you want?"

"It occurs to me, gentlemen," replied the tramp, "that it is not what I want, but what you want. However, since you are so kind as to put it that way, I will say, without delay, that I would like a drink."

The boys were immediately impressed with the reasonableness and good sense of this request, and Kingman poured out a grown man's supply, which the tramp seized eagerly and gulped down to the last drop.

"Now," said Mr. Ardway, winking at the boys, "p'r'aps you don't know that there is a law ag'in tramps in this town?"

The tramp smiled in a sickly manner that might have been a confession either of ignorance or indifference.

"Well, there is, a very good and just law. It passed this house ten minutes before your train got in, and it means death."

Still the tramp sat silent and unmoved. After a moment he spoke, with a sort of weary despondency of tone:

"I don't suppose it would make any difference to me or anybody else how soon death comes to me. I haven't long to live at the most, and a few days more or less don't matter."

Mr. Ardway gave the boys another wink. "I'm glad to see you resigned, and we'll make it as easy for you as we can. There ain't no particular hurry, and if there's anythin' you'd like to say or do special before we begin, you can go ahead."

The tramp looked listlessly about him. On the shelf behind the counter, just over George Blifer's head, was a violin. It belonged to Kingman's oldest boy, who played for his father's customers whenever they were musically inclined. A flash of joy came into the tramp's eyes, and he said, in a tone that was almost tender:

"I see a violin up there. It has been many months since I have held one in my hands. I think I should like to play again to-night."

"Oh, come off," said Mr. Chesney; "this ain't no musical conservatory."

"That's all right, Sam," interposed Mr. Ardway; "if he wants to give a concert it ain't gentlemanly to object." Then to the tramp: "We didn't know when we saw you gettin' off at our humble depot that you was a concert artist."

"I played the violin for many years," said the tramp, "when I was with Thomas."

"Oh, see here, what are you givin' us? There wasn't no violin-playing in the army, and you don't look as if you'd ever had spank enough to fight a rabbit."

The boys looked at Tom Hanks approvingly. Tom had a war record, and knew every division and brigade commander by name and history.

"I didn't say I ever was in the army," said the

tramp, humbly. "I meant that I played with Thomas, the orchestra leader, you know."

"Oh, that's different," grunted Mr. Hanks, and he looked at the boys as if to intimate that he was on personal terms with the Thomases of all creation.

"I was a happy fellow in those days, gentlemen," went on the tramp, almost caressing the fiddle that George handed to him. "It was back in New York, and I was young and ambitious. Perhaps you don't care for music. At all events, you've probably never played in a great orchestra with your blood tingling and a crash of harmony all around you."

"I'm sorry to say," put in Mr. Ardway, dryly, "as how most of us gave up our music when we were young, although we are reckoned right lively connysuers."

"It was glorious," said the tramp, without seeming to notice the apology. "Here stood Thomas, waving the baton, and here I sat at his left, in the first row of the violins. Down below me, and stretching back and to the right and to the left, is the brilliant audience, with eyes fastened on us, and not a rustle to disturb the music. We open with the overture to Rienzi."

The tramp had been tuning the instrument as he talked. Then he squared back and fiddled away with such rapidity and vehemence that the boys looked on astonished.

"Your teknéek seems to be all right," said Bill Cook, who had acquired a musical education at concerts in Dodge City, "but I ain't much stuck on that tune."

The criticism appeared to bring the tramp back to a realization of his position. He laid down the fiddle and sighed. "I don't know why it is, but when the fit strikes me I feel like playing a whole programme. But what's the use? If you don't have the brass and the reeds and the great volume behind you, how can you convey the grand inspiration of Wagner?"

"Sure," said Mr. Cook, who felt that his reputation demanded that he should say something.

"This may be very choice," broke in Mr. Chesney, impatiently, "but if you had such a soft snap why didn't you freeze to it?"

"That's just it," bitterly replied the tramp. "What did it? Why, whisky, of course. I don't preach any temperance sermon, but whisky cost me my place and reputation, set me adrift, brought me West, subjected me to hunger and cold and exposure, and brought on the disease that's about finished me. I was trying to get back home when the brakeman caught me. It was a chance anybody might take. The longing to go home was too strong to resist, and I thought if I could reach

Topeka I might find friends to help me. But perhaps it doesn't make any difference, for I can't last long, anyway."

If anybody had looked in Mr. Cook's face he would have seen a sort of twitching around the corners of Mr. Cook's mouth and a pitying expression in Mr. Cook's eyes. Mr. Ardway, too, had a much gentler tone when he said:

"It's the opinion of this meeting that your tunes are out of date. You ain't up to the times, and you ain't no credit to Kansas. It wouldn't be right to send you back without some signs of progress. Can't you play the Washerwoman's Dance or a heel and toe, or something with music in it?"

The tramp struck up a lively air, and the boys grinned and kept time with their feet on Kingman's barrels. Then the music came slower and slower, and the boot accompaniments stopped. The tramp's eyes were closed, and his mind had wandered again. It was a simple melody he played, but it touched the boys, and no city audience could have listened with more profound attention to the orchestra of which the tramp had been a part. Twice he played it with increasing fervor, and then he changed the theme and played, one after another, the airs that are popular in all sections of the country, and that, somehow, are always associated with home and childhood and better days. And old John Kingman listened in amazement. He could not believe that the beautiful tones he heard came from his boy's old fiddle. Still the tramp played on, until Captain Matthews, who sat near him, swore that he saw two tears come from his closed eyes and roll down his cheeks.

Sam Chesney drew a long breath. "That's the sort," said Mr. Chesney. Mr. Ardway held a hurried consultation with the Blilers and the Hanks boys and Bill Cook. Then he said, with great gravity:

"Stranger, it's the vote of this meeting that you've had a run of uncommon hard luck, and been imposed on by circumstances. If a man wants to go home and die, there ain't no kick coming to Elk Grove. So we've decided to make a pool and buy a ticket to Topeka, and start you off in style. Kingman's got a store-room back here, where there ain't nothing portable, and you can get a shakedown to-night and a square meal in the morning. You'll be expected to turn up after breakfast and fiddle us a few of them good old tunes, and we'll have the ladies down to hear you. Then we'll fix you out and flag the train and start you off."

If there was any doubt about the tears in the tramp's eyes when Cap. Matthews watched him, there was none now. "Believe me, gentlemen," he said, "I am not entirely unworthy of your kindness, even if I never repay you. I wasn't always what I am now, and what I am you can see I shall not be very long."

Mr. Chesney escorted the tramp to his lodging in the rear of the grocery, and Mr. Kingman and Mr. Ardway brought in a quilt and a pile of empty sacks, with an old army coat for a pillow. After the others had gone out Mr. Chesney lingered.

"I say, stranger," he said; "what was that tune you played just after the jig?"

The tramp pondered a moment. His face brightened. "That was the Ave Maria."

"What's the Avvy Mareea?" asked the puzzled Mr. Chesney.

"The Ave Maria," replied the tramp, "is a prayer to the Mother. I played it a hundred times when I was with Thomas."

Mr. Chesney helped old John lock up that night. Then the two men took the lantern and went around and looked in at the window. The tramp was lying on the quilts, and a peaceful look was on his thin face. Once he stirred and smiled in his sleep. "He thinks he's playing the Avvy Mareea," said Mr. Chesney.

And they tiptoed away, lest their presence might alarm the Mother.

Tubbs of Kansas.

TUBBS OF KANSAS.

EVERYBODY knew Tubbs. Along the line of the Santa Fé, from the old historic city of Lawrence, with its prim Puritan air, and its college atmosphere, far beyond Dodge City, where the playful cowboy "rounds up the tenderfoot," and disturbs the night with the joyous crack of the revolver, his name was a household word, and his deeds were a family lesson.

Tubbs was not a founder. He came from a long line of distinguished Tubbses, every one of them a Republican and every one a Methodist, "for which God in His infinite wisdom and mercy be praised," said Tubbs, with great unction.

More than thirty years ago Tubbs went to the first political convention at Topeka, and never thereafter missed a rally of the cohorts. "Forty years a voter, and, thank God, never a vote for a Democrat," said Tubbs. And a heavenly smile lighted up his face, and a sweet expression of rest gave evidence of the tranquil spirit within. The quality of Tubbs's Republicanism was not strained. At each succeeding political contest the old man enunciated his principles: "I'm for the nominee an' ag'in the Democratic party."

"What do you think about tariff reform?" anxiously asked a doubting neighbor.

"Is it in the platform?" queried Tubbs.

"No."

"Then I'm ag'in it. When you've lived in Kansas as long as I have, young man, and voted the straight Republican ticket as many years, you'll stand by the platform just as we used to stand by free soil in the dark days."

Whereat the party leaders would smile and say: "Yes, we can bank on Tubbs."

Tubbs lived in one of the outlying counties, a man of property and influence. He raised stock enough for his own uses, and his vast acres of corn and wheat smiled in every direction. By way of innocuous diversion he looked after the spiritual welfare of his neighbors at the periodic Methodist awakenings. And he read, as he had read for years, straight Republican literature, and was not quite positive in his own mind that the war was over, and that the rebels had been reduced to a proper state of subjection.

For social gayeties, in the general sense of the word, Tubbs cared little or nothing. "Dancing and such like frivolities," he was wont to say, "are ag'in the perfect letter of the law, and contrary to the teaching of the spirit." But Tubbs had married a woman who knew a thing or two about domestic discipline and was not disinclined to resent too close application of the doctrine of perfect holiness when it interfered with her worldly ambitions. For, although the country was new and society was in its formative stage, she already had aspirations to be recognized as the society leader of the county. So, when the new house was built, and the furniture had come from the city, she determined to give a ball that should settle the local leadership then and there. That ball is still the talk of the country roundabout, for Mrs. Tubbs, with a keen appreciation of the crisis, "laid herself out," as the local papers had it, and "accomplished a triumph worthy the best efforts of Lucullus." But at nine o'clock, as the festivities were beginning to alarm the wondering livestock, the mysterious absence of Tubbs was noted and whispered about. Search was instituted, and lantern parties organized, and the old man was at last discovered in the barn, fast asleep in the haymow. For, as he subsequently explained, "a working man has no business turning night into day, and caverting about on pleasure after nine o'clock." This mark of disapproval did in no way interfere with the pleasure of the merrymakers, but it vastly increased Tubbs's standing and power in the councils of the church.

One day the arch-tempter, who had been hanging around for years trying to get a good whack at Tubbs, came to him in the form of a neighbor, a late arrival, of Mugwumpish tendencies, and a Baptist, two reasons why Tubbs regarded him with suspicion and distrust. "You're all off on this tariff question, Tubbs," said the evil one. Tubbs smiled a little haughtily, but with certain Christian toleration, as prescribed by Wesleyan discipline.

"Of course," went on this wily tempter, "I don't mean to argue the matter with you, because I can't cope with you in argument, but if you don't mind, I'll just leave these papers and pamphlets with you and let you skin 'em over for yourself."

"If them are Democratic papers," said Tubbs suspiciously, "you can take 'em along. I ain't goin' to have the folks on this farm pizened by that kind of truck."

But later in the day Tubbs picked them up, "jest to see," he said, apologetically, to himself, "what the blamed fools have to say, anyhow." And from glancing he fell to reading, and from reading he went to thinking, and the result was that he sought his bed that night in great anguish of spirit.

From that fateful hour Tubbs felt that he was a changed man. And none was quicker to see it than the wily neighbor, who never talked politics, but who pursued his advantage by dexterously throwing tariff reform documents in Tubbs's way, and scattering Democratic and Mugwump papers over the farm where Tubbs could run across them without compromising his standing as an old John Brown Republican. And Tubbs read and thought, and read again, and his perplexity increased, and the dark shadow rested on his soul.

"It ain't right, Tilly," he said to his wife. "It's speshis, but it troubles me. It ain't good Methodist doctrine for Kansas, and it's ag'in all the glorious and blessed results of the war, but, dang me, if it doesn't seem like common sense."

"All this comes of trying to think for yourself," answered the wife, severely. "A man who helped put down the rebellion and gave one hundred dollars to build the first Methodist church in the county ain't got no business foolin' around with rebel newspapers."

"You're right, Tilly," said Tubbs, meekly, "but I can't quite make it out. If Plumb was here he could straighten me in ten minutes, and Barney Kelly could put me back in the fold, but 'my feet were almost gone and my steps had well nigh slipped.'"

Time passed. Tubbs kept his own counsel and prayed, with all the fervor of his strong nature, to be delivered from the snares of the tempter. He felt that he wasn't true to Kansas; that he was "goin' ag'in the platform;" that he was violating one of the cardinal principles of his life and political training, to vote the ticket and ask no questions. To add to his perplexity and unrest he was made chairman of the county delegation to Topeka, and he watched, with anguish, his wife as she laid out upon the bed his Prince Albert coat and black striped trousers, and carefully brushed his high hat of many years' service.

When Tubbs reached Topeka his first act was to call around at the Santa Fé general offices to pay his respects, in accordance with the unwritten law of delegates to the State convention. And, as he shook hands with the high officers of state, and heard their kind and affectionate inquiries as to himself and family, and received instructions for the approaching contest, he thought of his doubts and his hours of unbelief; of the heretical doctrine that he had devoured on the farm; and the still, small voice of conscience seemed to say: "Tubbs, you ain't true to your trainin'; you ain't true to Kansas."

In the cool of the evening Tubbs strolled about the town, uneasy and full of remorse. It seemed to him that every man on the street pointed a finger at him and cried: "There goes a traitor who thinks for himself!" Even the evolutions of the flambeau club and the stirring and beautiful songs of the Cyclones and Coyotes brought no diversion to his troubled spirit. And at nine o'clock he withdrew from the noisy throng and sought a little room on a back street, wherein he went hastily to bed and dreamed that he was the Benedict Arnold of the century and was delivering the country over to the English free-traders, to the great indignation of a highly protected ram, which was making for him with terrifying speed. And when he awoke in a great state of fear and perspiration it was four o'clock. And he arose and dressed, "for," says Tubbs, "I can't lay in the mornin'."

So Tubbs went down to the tavern, where he found the other members of the delegation sitting up against the office wall, waiting for the roosters to herald the advance of the king of day, and discussing a modification of the prohibition law to suit emergencies. To them, with evil and malicious intent, came a godless young man from a lost city in Missouri, and said: "Boys, I've got a prime article down in my grip." And with one accord those statesmen arose and shouted, "Where?"

When Tubbs had taken a long and steady pull he felt better. And after breakfast two or three of the leading railroad magnates and statesmen of Kansas dropped around and talked to him pleasantly and convincingly. Unburdening himself, he told of his troubles and his doubts. Then conversation became general, and Tubbs went upstairs and took another longer and steadier pull, and declared that he was ready for the conflict.

Looking at Tubbs in the convention hall it would have been difficult to recognize the sad,

troubled old man who left his farm perplexed
by free-trade pamphlets and tariff reform heresies.
Tubbs was in his element. The old Kansas
spirit was on him.

> "Again Marengo's field was won,
> And Jena's bloody battle."

Again he was ready to fight for John Brown,
or sheep, or tin plates, or cotton ties, or anything
else that might be suggested. Again he was surrounded
by congenial spirits, and again the
watchword was "Hooray!"

Tubbs fairly bubbled over with excitement.
And when it seemed that his enthusiasm must
have reached its height, the Coyotes, the sweet
singers of that glorious day and generation, came
forth and delivered themselves of a beautiful
patriotic melody, of which the concluding delicately
sentimental lines ran as follows:

> "When old Cleveland lays him down to die,
> And sees this grand army in the sky,
> He'll have nothing to do but roast and fry—
> Keep in the middle of the road."

"Hooray!" shouted Tubbs. "Glory, hallelujah!"

The burst of enthusiasm excited by this fine bit
of typical Kansas poetry having subsided, Tubbs
arose and called upon that grand statesman and
powerful advocate, Mr. Hamfat, to "address the
meetin'." Mr. Hamfat came forward with alacrity.
He had made the question of the tariff a life-long

study, and was prepared to demolish all unfriendly criticism.

"When," said Mr. Hamfat, "the hour of twelve has come, the American workingman uncovers his dinner-pail — protected dinner-pail — and takes out a slice of fresh, white American bread — protected bread."

"Hooray!" shouted Tubbs.

"Then he brings out a nice roll of fresh country American butter — protected butter."

"Hooray!" yelled Tubbs.

"Then he draws forth a fine large slice of American beef — protected beef."

"Hooray! hooray!" gasped Tubbs.

"Ha! what have we here?" exclaimed Mr. Hamfat, peering theatrically into space, and clutching the air as if the dinner pail danced before him. "Pie!"

Tubbs tumbled in a fit, and the convention went wild. Whoever has not seen a Kansas political gathering in a moment of enthusiasm can have little idea of the excitement of that climax. Banners and handkerchiefs were waved in every part of the hall, the band played "Rally Round the Flag," and the delegates stood on their chairs and cheered, and sang, and whooped, and shed tears, and behaved altogether in a highly boisterous and indecorous manner. Tariff reform, agitation of months, was upset by that one word "pie." Mr. Hamfat's logic had wrought its perfect work. What mattered the trifling formality of platform or ticket to those statesmen who were cheering for "pie"? Mr. Hamfat descended with the lofty assurance of a man who has driven the last nail in the coffin of argument.

And that was the last of Tubbs as a rational being. From that moment he sang, and danced, and whooped, and indorsed everybody and everything. He heard the firing on Sumter for the nineteenth time. He railed at the Democratic party, and he drew such frightful pictures of Bacchanalian orgies at the White House under a Democratic administration that even the experienced superintendent of the State insane asylum came over and watched him with professional curiosity and solicitude. And he moved that every candidate be nominated by acclamation, and that the platform be adopted without reading, and fell on Brother Kelly's neck and wept, and said: "I was as a sheep gone astray, but I have returned to the fold, and have consecrated my life anew."

But they put Tubbs on a way freight and sent him home, where he was received by Tilly with feminine sniffs of suspicion and certain forcible expressions of disapproval. And some hours later, when in a measure he had calmed down, Tubbs remarked, apologetically:

"Tilly, it does a feller a powerful heap o' good to go up to Topeky and hear the perlitical issues ably discussed."

How the Lord Remembered Curly.

HOW THE LORD REMEMBERED CURLY.

It was three o'clock in the afternoon, and there was a small commotion in Star Alley. The new boy had come around to get his papers. True, in the general cut and fit of the new boy's clothes there was nothing iconoclastic. His trousers were decidedly in the nature of the prevailing style of the young men of his class, being much too short in the legs and considerably too spacious in the seat and at the knees. His shoes bore the aspect of having been married, not mated, and the toe-ends thereof seemed to threaten a general eruption. His shirt was unpretentious enough to disarm Arabian hostility, and the coat that loosely covered it could not in any way be accepted as a reflection on the taste of his companions. In fact, on the principle that a well-dressed boy is the boy whose dress excites no comment, the new-comer was, in the judgment of the alley, a well-dressed boy.

But when Micky Finn, who was the acknowledged leader of "de gang," called attention to the new boy's hair, there was a general murmur of disapprobation. Indeed, this hair was quite a revelation in its way. It was fair and soft and hung in curls down to his shoulders, each curl standing out as if a mother had lovingly twisted it in her fingers. And it was this hair that gave great offense to the motley company waiting for the first edition, and caused such rude exclamations and personal interrogations as "Ketch on to de freak!" "Look at mamma's pet!" "It's one of de seven Sutherland sisters!" "Why don't it go to de musyum?" accompanied by certain swaggering motions of a threatening nature.

The new boy was not in the least abashed or intimidated by this outcry, but stood blinking lazily at the crowd with a look on his face that was construed by Micky Finn as far-away, and, therefore, insulting to an eminent degree. Micky bristled up.

"Who curled your hair?" he asked.

"My mother," answered the new boy, calmly.

It was a respectful answer, but Micky didn't like it. He came a little nearer and said, threateningly:

"You'll have to cut it."

"I sha'n't," said the new boy.

A gasp went through the crowd. It was the first open rebuke the leader of the gang had received since he laid Tommy Timmins low. Micky himself was a little dazed at the bold impertinence. He stepped up briskly and slapped the new boy in the face. For a minute there was a confusion of legs and arms and boots and curls, and from the dust arose wails from Micky, who was receiving in all parts of his small anatomy painful punches from the vigorous fists of "mamma's pet." And when one of the pressmen ran out and pulled off the new boy the Finn dynasty had perished. The king was dead. Long live the king!

It is only just to the new boy to say that he bore his honors with becoming humility, and accepted the crown and the succession with no trace of undue exhilaration. He told the committee of notification, Patsy Haley and Reddy Dobbs, that his mother called him Jamie, and he admitted, very frankly, that he didn't like the name. But the boys had already dubbed him Curly, and Curly he shall be to the end of this chapter.

As the days went by Curly grew in the confidence and esteem of the gang. Even Micky was his stanch lieutenant. And one night when the leader of the opposition crowd offered to wipe Curly off the face of the earth, Micky then and there threw himself into the breach as a vicarious sacrifice. But Curly refused to be deprived of his prerogatives, and with great ardor and almost unseemly haste he thrashed his incautious challenger, and transferred the championship to "de West Side."

In all projects for mental recreation and improvement Curly was the leading spirit. After the papers were off and sold he would put himself at the head of the gang and pilot the way to the Varieties, where Mlle. Spaghetti, the charming queen of song, was a stellar attraction of the first magnitude. And there he and his companions would sit through the performance, munching peanuts and other nutritious luxuries, listening critically to the musical numbers and commenting in the hearty, unbiased way of the juvenile connoisseur. And after the show they would repair to their favorite chop-house, which they designated by the somewhat misleading title "de club," and partake of such viands as only a boy's stomach can successfully withstand.

There was great excitement in Star Alley when the play-bills announced that, in consequence of an imperative demand for her presence in the East, prior to her return to Paris, Mlle. Spaghetti would take a positively final farewell benefit. The manager begged leave to announce that for this occasion, by superhuman efforts and at fabulous expense, he had engaged the services of Mlle. Natalie, the world's greatest skirt-dancer. He also desired to add, incidentally, that with a reckless, almost fatal, disregard of the terrible financial risk involved, he had stipulated for the appearance of Zuleika, the peerless Mistress of the Air, who would leap from a flying trapeze and turn three distinct somersaults before alighting in the net. Other startling attractions would be offered in addition to the great charm of the beneficiary herself, who would not only sing her wonderful creation, "La Paloma," but would appear in her most dazzling protean specialties.

In the interval between the sale of the first edition and the appearance of the second, Curly called a meeting of the gang and announced that the fraternity would be expected to honor the great Spaghetti in a body. He argued with great earnestness that the gang had always encouraged true and conscientious art, and he submitted that the efforts of the manager in catering broadly and liberally to an advanced popular taste merited marked and substantial recognition. These remarks, which are generalized with only the faintest suggestion of Curly's eloquence, were greeted with great enthusiasm and indorsed by a full bench.

It was, therefore, with the utmost surprise that on the afternoon preceding the only Spaghetti's farewell triumph the boys in the alley noted the absence of Curly. The last edition, and then the postscript, came out on the street, and still the leading patron of art was missing. At a quarter before eight there was a call of the roll at the usual rendezvous, and all responded save one. That one was Curly. With heavy hearts the gang filed into the theater, and took its elevated position of honor. But the entertainment had been robbed of its chief glory. In vain the erstwhile Queen of Song warbled her most bewitching lyrics. In vain the peerless Natalie shook her skirts and disported to the pleasing strains of the augmented orchestra. Gloom reigned in the critics' corner, and, finally, when the lithe Zuleika swung gracefully from the trapeze, the disgusted Patsy Haley stood up and bade her, in tones of wrathful scorn, "come off de perch." That was exactly what she intended to do, but so disconcerted was the Mistress of the Air by the shrill, piping command that she came off too soon, and instead of turning three distinct somersaults, as per three-sheets, she landed a confused, disheveled and disgraced mass in the outstretched net, and the boys, with many cutting expressions of ribaldry and wrath, went over to the club and banqueted in solemn silence. And the consensus of opinion gathered then and there was that the benefit had been a failure, and that the beautiful Spaghetti was an "old stiff."

Another day passed, and Curly had neither appeared nor sent word of comfort. The gang was becoming demoralized, and there were indications of an onslaught from the Philistines of the East side. Micky Finn rose up to meet the emergency.

He admitted that Curly might be wrestling with diphtheria or even contending against scarlet fever, but something had to be done right away. So, having disposed of his papers at a slaughter sale, he summoned Patsy Haley and Reddy Dobbs and organized a committee of investigation.

Curly and his widowed mother occupied unpretentious apartments in a well-filled tenement-house at a convenient distance from the madding crowd. For purposes of ventilation and other reasons, hygienic and economic, these apartments were at a considerable distance above the telegraph wires, and commanded a fine view of the packing-house district and the bend of the Missouri River where it travels away from Kansas at a regular speed of four miles an hour. The boys knew little of Curly's mother beyond the fact that she was a sewing-woman with strong religious tendencies which, thus far, had not been transmitted to her son. However, so great was the awe inspired by the very thought of a person with authority over Curly that they had no sooner climbed the three narrow flights leading to Curly's suite than their courage failed them. They paused at the end of the long, gloomy hall and emitted those peculiar sounds by which a boy signifies to another boy that he is wanted.

Great was the satisfaction of the gang when the door opened and Curly's head protruded. Then Curly's body followed, and directly Curly's legs carried him down the hall to his lieutenants, by whom he was received with fitting demonstration of affection.

"Wot's de matter, Curly?" asked Micky.

"Mother's sick."

"Well, ain't yer had no doc?"

"No."

"Why ain't yer had no doc?" demanded Patsy Haley, sternly.

"Because," answered Curly, desperately, "I ain't had no money. First it was de rent, and den it was t'ings to eat, and we got broke before we knowed it."

A faint voice called from the chamber, and Curly disappeared with more rapidity than he had come. The boys looked at one another, and Micky blurted out:

"How much yer got, Patsy?"

"T'irty-t'ree cents."

"How much yer got, Reddy?"

"Twenty-four cents."

"And I've got forty-one cents. Dat makes ninety-eight cents ter pay for a doc fer Curly's mudder. We owe it to him, anyhow. When my dog was took up Curly paid ter git him out. When you got stuck on der extry papes, Reddy, Curly took 'em off yer hands. When Patsy lost all his money on craps Curly paid for his supper and took him to der te-ayter. So we'll hire de doc."

"But no doc ain't goin to come fer no ninety-eight cents," scornfully said Reddy.

"Wot's de reason he ain't?" replied Micky. "De boom is off, and docs is liable ter come fer wot dey can get. An' I knows one dat'll come anyhow. It's Doc Streator. I seed him out at de ball game Sunday afternoon, an' he's de right stuff."

Doctor Streator sat in his office discussing Presidential possibilities with a friend. It had been a prosperous day with the doctor, and he felt convivial and friendly. And when he said "Come in," and three small and not over-prepossessing boys entered, he was more cordial than might have been expected.

"Well, what do *you* want?"

"We want yer to come and see a sick woman," said Micky.

"How much money have you got?"

"Ninety-eight cents."

"You don't suppose I'm going down into the footpad district for ninety-eight cents, do you?"

Micky grinned. "Yer said yer'd go any time I asked yer."

"I did, eh? When did I say that?"

"Out at de ball game one Sunday afternoon."

The doctor's friend leaned back and laughed. "So you patronize Sunday ball games, do you, Streator? Tell us about it, kid."

"It was de great game between Minneapolis and

Kansas City fer de championship," said Micky. "Me an' Curly an' Reddy here an' Patsy had made a sneak over de fence when de cops wasn't lookin'. De grand-stand an' bleachers was all full, an' de people was pourin' down inter de field. We stood near de doc an' two or t'ree udder swells in de nint' innin' when Minneapolis was two runs ahead."

"Yes, I remember that inning," said the doctor.

"Gunny came ter de bat," resumed Micky, "an' made a hit. Den Swartzell, what can't hit a balloon mostly, knocked one over de second bag. An' Holland hit a slow one inter de infield, an' de muckers was so excited dat dey tumbled all over it, an' Gunny come home. Den little Nic sent anudder easy one, an' he an' Holland got put out on de double play. About dis time Round-de-World Jimmy he gits foxy an' waits, an' gits a base on balls. An' everybody was so excited dat dey breaks inter de diamon' an' hollers an' yells, an' Elmer Smith a-standin' at de plate, swingin' his bat an' waitin' fer a good one. An' I seed de doc a-wavin' his hat an' hollerin' with de rest of 'em. De Minneapolis pitcher got rattled, an' it was ten minutes before de cops could get de doc an' de rest back inter line, while dey kep' on hollerin': 'Hit 'er out, Elmer!' An' fin'ly Elmer got one just where he wanted it, an' hit 'er out fer t'ree bags, way ter de center-field fence, an' Swartzell an' Jimmy come streakin' in, an' we knowed de game was won. An' we all broke inter de diamon' ag'in an' turned flip-flaps an' hollered. An' de doc was jumpin' around an' flingin' his arms, an' he hit me chug in de eye. An' den he gave me ten cents an' told me dat if I ever wanted him I should call on him an' say: 'Minneapolis.'"

The doctor threw himself back and chuckled at the reminiscence, and his friend opened his mouth and showed such a wide expanse of palate, and laughed so uproariously, that the three boys fell back in evident alarm. The doctor was the first to recover.

"As a man of my word," said he, "I must see this thing through. Come on, boys; we'll go and take a look at the 'mudder.'"

"And I'll go along, too," said his friend. "Perhaps here is an opportunity for genuine philanthropy. Don't you worry about the bill, boys," he added, kindly; "I'll look after that myself."

"Dat's de room; de t'ird one to de left," whispered Micky, as the party stopped to breathe on the third landing. And as the two gentlemen knocked on the door, he drew the other boys aside and said, decisively:

"Yer heered de doc's friend say dat Curly's mudder ought to have some delic'cies. Wot's de matter wid our gittin' 'em?"

The proposition struck the boys favorably, for

the idea that a gentleman could in any way rise to an appreciation of delicacies, as the poorer classes understood them, was altogether too absurd to be encouraged or entertained.

The doctor was saying, "Merely a case of debility and low fever, brought on by over-work and insufficient and improper nourishment," when the three boys entered the room, bearing burdens of tribute.

"What's that?" he asked, sharply.

"Dem's delic'cies," answered Micky, with pride and confidence.

"For the Lord's sake, look here, Streator!" said his friend. And he drew forth first a cold pig's-foot, then a tin saucepan of beans with a huge chunk of pork in the middle, half a jelly-cake, three or four greasy crullers, a Vienna sausage, liberally sprinkled with horse-radish, and a lemon pie. Curly was visibly affected by these unmistakable evidences of affection, and his eyes rested lovingly on the pie.

"For a low fever," said the doctor, thoughtfully, "I cannot conscientiously recommend this sort of diet." And as the boys' faces fell, he added: "A little quiet celebration in the hall in the way of a supper for this young man here doesn't seem to be out of the way."

So the boys took Curly into the passageway and stuffed him full of beans and pigs'-feet and jelly-cake and lemon pie, and told him of the disgrace that had overtaken the Mistress of the Air, and related the thousand and one things that had upset the alley since his departure, and unfolded a sinister plot to do up the other gang as soon as he was able to assume the command.

And the doctor talked cheerily to the mother, and promised to have her up and out in three days. And his friend left a five-dollar bill on the table, and intimated that other tokens of a friendly interest would be speedily forthcoming. And the poor mother, being a very weak and foolish woman, could only cry softly and mumble a few inarticulate words about the blessing of Heaven, which the two gentlemen did not, or pretended they did not, hear.

But when the whole party had gone off down the stairs the mother called Curly to her, and ran her fingers through his tangled hair, and said: "I told you, Jamie, that the Lord would remember those who trust in Him. You will not forget to thank Him and bless His name."

Curly went to the window. Far down in the street three sturdy little figures were trudging along, the happiness in their big hearts banishing the remembrance of their empty pockets. And he turned to the sick mother and said, simply:

"An' de gang, mother, de gang!"

The Involuntary Marriage.

THE INVOLUNTARY MARRIAGE.

NEARLY forty years ago, when Thomas Benton, in a spirit of prophecy and a premonition of brilliant futurity, had pointed to the Pacific Ocean and exclaimed: "There is the east, there is India!" the restless fortune-seekers had begun to drift into Kansas. Some passed on to the mountains, others to the far-away gold-fields of California, while the more prudent and conservative remained where the well-watered and fertile valleys promised fields of golden cereals more attractive and less illusive than the precious metal of the new El Dorado. Many of these people are living to-day, less adventurous, less hazard-loving than when they first crossed the Missouri River, but full of that same spirit and impulse that made a Kansas possible. If they have lost their youth they have not lost their pride in the memory of their youth, and the tales they relate and the incidents they recall are full of the quaint humor that adds delight to the recital.

There were cranks in those days, the wildest, maddest, most hopeless cranks; cranks of every shade and every tendency: cranks in religious belief and in social customs; cranks that criticised the Lord and defied the devil; cranks in politics and in art; cranks in manner and in dress. And they all seemed to come together by a common impulse and to move into Kansas.

That one crank should tolerate another was the very essence of the true spirit of liberty. It was a sort of chivalrous idea of freedom entirely consistent with the American spirit of progress, and was founded on the conviction that time would make the test and prove all things. Tim Murphy exemplified this spirit. Tim had drifted into Kansas in search of adventure, and, in one way and another, had found it until he settled down in the reposeful dignity of a saloon-keeper. His tremendous strength and his fighting qualities added greatly to his reputation, and, as he had thrashed every pretender in the neighborhood, he was much admired and respected. One day, while helplessly intoxicated, he insulted a little Irishman, who took advantage of his condition and knocked him down between two whisky barrels. As often as Tim would essay to rise, his small opponent would hit him on the nose and tumble him back. At last the bystanders interfered and held the little man, whereupon Tim exclaimed, with maudlin dignity: "Lave him be; lave him be, and let him sweat himself to death knockin' me down."

This anecdote illustrates the tolerant spirit of

the Kansan toward his associates, granted, perhaps, in every instance save the one never-forgotten and never-forgiven sin, slavery and pro-slavery sentiment.

Into this strange jumble of social conditions came Daniel Eastmann and his wife forty years ago. A queer old couple, with much of the sternness of the Puritan and the vigor and aggressiveness of the modern Yankee in their composition. Unhappily, however, a little of the recognized austere morality of the Puritan character was lacking, as duly appeared. The Eastmanns were not at the age when people look about for new homes to be acquired only by ceaseless toil and with threatening ills. But the old man was strong and active, and capable of immense labors, and his wife stood up under her share of the responsibilities with no betrayal of weakness or disappointment. They had pushed on to the westward in their search for an abiding-place, and, finding nothing that promised contentment, had returned to Kansas and settled down to the ordinary details of pioneer life in one of the best and most prosperous of the Kansas settlements. They were good-natured, easy-going folk, and as they minded their own business in a strictly legitimate way, they were looked upon as no undesirable additions to the community. For it was one of the privileges of the time that the people in the main were too busy with their own affairs to waste the hours gossiping about their neighbors.

Little by little, however, the rumor went around that, notwithstanding the decorous behavior of old man Eastmann and his partner, and despite the undisputed nature of their relations, the couple had never been married. The women were the first to discover this delicate social question, and to express their regret that in the hurry to get along in life the old people had overlooked this trifling formality. The men shrugged their shoulders and remarked that that was "Eastmann's business," and if Mrs. Eastmann was satisfied it was not necessary to put too fine a point on the amicable domestic arrangement. Moreover, they had no children; therefore, no damage could be done except in the way of example, and as long as the example was merely tolerated, not indorsed, it would, doubtless, end right there.

For this magnanimous sentiment the old gentleman did not evince any surprising amount of gratitude. When he learned that his "arrangement" had been subjected to discussion and, in instances, to criticism, he boldly acknowledged the state of affairs. He called attention to the agitated condition of American society, to the numerous crazes that were affecting the people, and intimated that he had as much right to his whim as other people had to theirs. Furthermore, with him it was strictly a matter of conscience, and he flattered himself that he had at last come to a part of the country where individual conscience counted for a great deal.

This compliment to Kansas pleased the community immensely. Moreover, it was not to be denied that the delicate reminder as to "other people's whims" smacked of a truth that was irrefutable. So the little peculiarity was passed over as an innocuous fancy, and the Eastmanns were firmly established as a part of the social fabric. Occasionally the old man would partake too freely of the popular liquor of the day, and at such times would discourse eloquently on the iniquitous marriage laws of the United States, but these orations merely amused the neighbors, and did not in the least detract from his standing or debar him from the privileges of social gayeties.

One night the Perkinses gave an entertainment of unusual brilliancy, and as Perkins was somewhat of a crank himself he made it a special point that all the other cranks should be present. Inasmuch as the cranks, of one kind or another, composed four-fifths of the population, it is easy to imagine that the hospitable home of the Perkinses was the theater of a large and brilliant collection of human freaks. The Eastmanns were conspicuous among the guests, not only through reason of their entertaining social qualities, but on account of the exhilarating amount of liquor which the old man carried where he felt it would do him the most good. He was in an argumentative mood also, and the marriage laws of the country were shown to be unjust and inhuman in every corner of Perkins's house.

The Rev. Mr. Duncan looked upon Eastmann with sorrow stamped on his benevolent face. Mr. Duncan was a holy man. He endeavored, by his godly life as well as by his spiritual exhortation, to bring his people into the strait and narrow path and keep them there. The peculiar relation of the Eastmanns had always been to this worthy man the source of sincere grief and perplexing thought. How to influence them to a realization of their offense against Christian morality and the enlightened spirit of the age was the problem that consumed many of his moments. Eastmann, fond as he was of argument and of defending his theories, could never be brought to face Parson Duncan. If they met on the street, the old man hurried on with a half-respectful nod. If the preacher halted before his gate, Eastmann slipped out of the back door. To outsiders it appeared that the old man was afraid of the parson, but Eastmann excused himself on the ground that preachers had no sense and weren't worth talking to. So matters had run along for months, and apparently Parson Duncan was as far away from all hope of practical good as ever.

When the parson looked around the Perkinses' rooms and saw the Eastmanns, something told him that the hour had come. A social gathering is not exactly the place for earnest missionary work, but Parson Duncan went on the theory that he must do his Master's bidding at any time or place, according as it is written: "Whatsoever thy hand findeth to do, do it with thy might." In this cheerful and godly resolution he was favored by circumstances. Eastmann stood in the corner of the room with a dozen grinning friends around him. He discoursed on his favorite theme: liberty of action and liberty of conscience; and what he lacked in argument he made up in declamation and gesture. The parson quietly edged his way into the circle, adjusted his spectacles, and listened. And when the parson looked over his spectacles, it was a trying and a critical moment for the devil and the instruments of his mischief.

The old man scowled. Plainly, he was annoyed by the parson's presence. Truly, the goodness that shone round about that righteous man was a constant menace to even the smallest impropriety, and a perpetual rebuke. But there was no dodging the issue. He must go ahead or strike his colors, and to a man of Eastmann's pride and doggedness surrender was out of the question. Indeed, after the first surprise, he was gratified to note that he was more fluent than usual, and with his renewal of courage came a wealth of sarcasm and a fund of wit that delighted his hearers and provoked many outbursts of laughter. Mrs. Eastmann, standing near, took no part in the conversation, but her smiles showed her appreciation of the old man's argument and her sympathy with his opinions.

Parson Duncan was not a joker. Perhaps he never willingly made a jest in his life, and as for sarcasm, his gentle nature abhorred it. But he was simple, and earnest, and straightforward, and he never shrank from any contest that might seem to lie within his duty. So when old Eastmann had finished he took up the subject in his thoughtful, considerate way, and argued the responsibility of the individual to society, and the necessity of uniformity in a perfect moral system. Furthermore, he quoted freely from the Scriptures, instanced the divine blessing on the marriage tie, and dwelt on the solemnity and beauty of the marriage ceremony with such fervor that Mrs. Eastmann cast down her eyes, and others standing around were visibly affected.

The news that Parson Duncan and old Eastmann had at last locked horns spread with great rapidity, and in a moment the guests had crowded into the room where the discussion was at heat. Eastmann's perversity and obstinacy increased with the size of his audience. He held the good parson's words up to ridicule in a manner that reflected great credit on his powers at repartee, but to the disadvantage of his standing as a respecter of the cloth. The parson's troubled face showed that he was pained by Eastmann's levity, and when he spoke again his tone was more decisive, and boded no good for the enemy of the altar.

"It is really strange, very strange," said Parson Duncan. "I cannot, even from your argument, understand your aversion to the marriage ceremony, as sanctioned by your country. You tell me that you love this woman with whom you are living."

"I don't deny that," answered old Eastmann, with a grin.

"And you tell me further that you expect to live with her as long as you are on earth, as every husband is expected to do."

"That has always been my intention, and I guess I'll stick to it."

The parson stood a minute, absorbed in thought. "Remarkable, very remarkable," he muttered. Then, turning abruptly to the woman, and speaking gently to her for the first time, he asked:

"Can it be true that you love this man who has done you a wrong, or at least has encouraged you in a false and unworthy belief?"

The woman showed her confusion, and lowered

her eyes. Recovering herself, she looked at the parson steadily, and said:

"I have always loved him, sir."

"And do you, in the face of this error, hope and expect to live with him all your life?"

"Oh, yes, sir."

"Then," exclaimed the holy man, with a ring of triumph in his voice and a heightened color on his face, "by virtue of my office, and in accordance with the laws that govern this Territory, I pronounce you man and wife. Kiss your bride, sir!"

Colonel Bollinger.

COLONEL BOLLINGER.

DISPUTE it who may, contradict it who will, the fact remains that the Ancient and Honorable Order of Colonels has been for many years the pride and glory of the people of the land of Corn. How and where this order originated has never been explained to the entire satisfaction of the Colonels themselves. Some historians and archæologists have claimed that it was introduced into Missouri by Colonel Daniel Boone when he left Kentucky in a huff in 1795, and that Colonel Boone had formed the parent chapter in Kentucky three years before. Others assert that the modern Colonel did not exist, either by right of heritage or of knighthood, until after Missouri had been incorporated as a State. A third faction contends that the order sprang into existence shortly after the Mexican War, but achieved no prominence as a political or social factor until the close of the operations in 1860-65. Be all this as it may, the order has attained a remarkable growth, and now numbers thousands of members in Missouri and Kansas, to say nothing of the branches in other States and Territories. Perhaps next to the Louisville chapter, the Kansas City chapter is the most famous, both for its aggregation of wealth, culture and courtliness, and for the display of those shining social qualities which differentiate the true Colonel from his fellow-man.

To guard against all possible misapprehension it must be said that Doctor Webster's definition of "Colonel" is very misleading. The Colonel, as understood in the Missouri interpretation of the word, is not the leader of a regiment or of a column, and, in fact, has no martial pretensions whatever. Nor is the word used in the old English sense and in the vulgar manner described by Samuel Butler in *Hudibras*. The Missouri Colonel is indeed a leader, but a leader of men and measures in a purely civil or social way. A clearer idea of this distinction may be gained from a queer little pamphlet which was discovered in one of the old slave counties of central Missouri some years ago. This pamphlet purported to give the constitution and by-laws of the Order of Colonels, and, although it has never been officially acknowledged, it cannot be denied that it is wonderfully faithful to appearances. Herein it is alleged that the order is a social, not a business organization, and that business meetings are strictly prohibited save in moments of rare emergency. The restrictions bearing on membership are thus set down:

"Article I. Section 1. Once a Colonel, always a Colonel.

"Section 2. No person who has participated in military service shall be eligible to membership.

"Section 3. In time of war the Colonel shall prepare for peace.

"Section 4. The pen is mightier than the sword, and the pruning-hook has distinct advantages over the spear.

"Section 5. Drink no longer water, but use a little stimulant for thy stomach's sake."

Colonel Bollinger had been a Colonel for so many years that it was popularly believed that he was born that way. Indeed, Colonel Bollinger himself smiled amiably and mysteriously whenever the question was introduced in his presence. He lived on a handsome estate near the city, and rode a fine dapple-gray mule into town whenever affairs of state were pressing. For the Colonel was quite an oracle in his way, and his opinions were widely sought, not only by his fellow-Colonels, but by people of all conditions in life, more especially political life. And while, as a lawyer, Colonel Bollinger might have acquired great wealth by the sale of his opinions, such was his overflowing good nature that he would sit all day in front of a popular caravansary, dispensing advice to all comers, free as salvation, and pausing only for a few moments on motion to adjourn to an excellent

place of refreshment in high favor with the
Colonels. And at night, well pleased with a day
profitably spent, and a trifle top-heavy from
excessive good cheer, he would mount the dapple-
gray mule and jog leisurely homeward, distribut-
ing pleasant greetings and delivering appropriate
orations by the way.

Colonel Bollinger found great delight in the
society of Colonel Dunklin, with whom he had
daily many convivial bouts and justs at knightly
repartee. Colonel Bollinger was much more impressive than Colonel Dunklin, being of full habit,
with great abdominal capacity, and with a voice
that on occasion could roar as fiercely as the Gae-
tulian lion or "as gently as the sucking dove."
Colonel Dunklin, on the other hand, had all the
mild outer characteristics of the typical Missouri
Colonel. He was tall and willowy. His hair was
rather long, and his eyes were full of pathos. He
wore the black slouch hat of the brigadier, the
long black coat, the shiny trousers with the broad
flares that covered the tight-fitting boots, the vest
open down to the last button, the high collar and
the shoe-string necktie. Without he was the picture of melancholy and humility, but inwardly, it
was whispered among the Colonels, he was full of
dead men's bones.

One fine day, as was their wont on all days,
regardless of meteorological conditions, Colonel

Bollinger and Colonel Dunklin were proceeding arm in arm down the street with a certain little back room as the definite object in view. Colonel Bollinger was in an extraordinary flow of spirits, and his cheery oratory excited the smiles and the admiration of the people who paused to salute the Colonels and receive, perchance, a sort of benediction in return. Turning a corner rather sharply, the Colonels were suddenly precipitated into the arms of Mr. Tubbs of Kansas, who had come down to the city in the interest of prohibition, of which theory he was one of the most earnest apostles. A moment of profound embarrassment followed, for in the campaign of the previous fall Colonel Bollinger had made a few Democratic speeches in Tubbs's neighborhood, and in the excitement of debate had likened Tubbs to several pleasing varieties of the *Mephitis Americana*, or domestic skunk. To which Tubbs had replied with spirit, repelling the implied family connection, and stigmatizing the Colonel as a vampire, a hyena, a buzzard, and several other birds and animals with carnivorous proclivities. The incident had been taken up by the party newspapers, and had led to a violent denunciation of Colonel Bollinger, who was berated throughout the State of Kansas as an ex-rebel brigadier, a guerrilla, and a bushwhacker, much to the detriment of his standing as a Colonel.

Colonel Bollinger first recovered presence of

mind. With a sweep of his arm which arrested the attention of the passers-by, and with a tone of the most engaging sweetness, he said:

"Ah, this must be Colonel Tubbs, of Kansas. I am glad to see you in old Mizzoora, sir. Allow me to make you acquainted with Colonel Dunklin, one of the old guard, sir."

And before the still embarrassed Tubbs could reply he went on:

"When we last met, Colonel Tubbs, over in your country, sir, we had a passage at arms. According to the brutalities of life we should still be enemies, but I cannot forget, sir, that you are now in my territory, and the laws of hospitality forbid. I may add that I am glad, sir, that we are so happily met. My friend Colonel Dunklin and I were stepping down for a little refreshment. Will you join us? You must join us."

Tubbs offered a feeble resistance and surrendered. Moreover, it was now high noon, and Tubbs was weary and dry. The three gentlemen passed down the street, turned one corner, then another, and disappeared behind a door which was familiar to every Colonel in at least two States. They passed unflinchingly by the elegantly polished counter and into the room beyond.

The little old gentleman who was expectantly taking down three tumblers stared at them in astonishment. "I have been in business a good many years," said he confidentially to his assistant, "and I have had considerable experience with the Colonels, from whom I derive not a little of my princely revenue, but this is the first time that I ever saw any of them pass this counter without weakening."

"Colonel Tubbs," said Colonel Bollinger, as the gentlemen sat down at the table, "if I am not deceived in the habit of you Kansas gentlemen, it must be hours since you breakfasted." Then, addressing the negro waiter: "George, take the gentleman's order."

Tubbs began to feel a little more at ease. "If you don't mind," said he, half apologetically, "I think I will try a whitefish. Not that we don't have fish in our country," he added, hastily, "for our channel cat is considered mighty good eatin', but a whitefish, with a little whisky on the side"—here Tubbs lowered his voice—"is my favor-ite meal."

"Good, very good," replied Colonel Bollinger, approvingly. "A whitefish is excellent eating, especially with whisky, which destroys its fat and deleterious qualities. George, bring a whitefish and a whisky—no, stop, a whitefish and three whiskies, and two plates of bacon and greens, and have three more whiskies ready on call."

All this time Colonel Dunklin sat in silence, with his pathetic eyes fastened upon a placard on the wall, the letters standing out with a clear-cut cameo distinctness, and forming the expressive and suggestive sentence: "Lunch without drinks, 20 cents."

"I don't suppose that it is right for me," said Colonel Dunklin, dreamily, "to dictate to a man how he shall run his business, and I don't think that twenty cents is too much for a lunch, if the lunch is clean, well cooked and palatable. But what bothers me is how anybody in the possession of reasoning faculties can want a lunch without drinks."

"As for that matter," replied Colonel Bollinger, "it seems absurd, from a mere financial standpoint, that a man should pay twenty cents for a lunch and a drink when he can get two drinks and a lunch thrown in for a quarter. The longer you remain with us, Colonel Tubbs, the better you will understand these grasping tricks of the trade."

The whitefish and the Missouri sauce had diffused a gentle glow through Tubbs's system, and had put him on friendly, almost bold, terms with his companions. "I should like to be a Colonel very much indeed," he said, heartily, "but the fact is I only got to be a captain in the war"—

At the word "war" the Colonels turned very pale and laid down their knives, shuddering violently. But Tubbs, not perceiving, went on:

"The question is, if I became a Colonel, as I

want to, ain't I likely to lose my standin' as a prohibitionist?"

"Our attitude," answered Colonel Bollinger, "is easily understood. It is always our intention, so long as God gives us the strength, to throw our influence against the ravages of prohibition. You are undoubtedly conscientious in the stand you have taken — George. fill up the gentleman's glass — but we contend that all sumptuary laws are calculated to strike a blow at the fundamental principles of our system. While the personal liberty of speech should be in no sense abridged, we cannot, as a body, interfere with the inequalities of the law in other communities, except as pertains to personal welfare and comfort."

"You should, however, at all times," interrupted Colonel Dunklin, "be well fortified against these inequalities."

"Of course," said Colonel Bollinger, earnestly, "that is understood. And so I would advise you to be what we might call a non-resident Colonel, submit as patiently as possible, and continue to procure inspiration in the facile way now popular in Kansas. I admire you, sir; I admire any man for devotion to principle, however mistaken. George. bring me three lumps of sugar and a very little water. I will show you, sir, how to make an excellent Kentucky toddy."

As Tubbs sipped the intoxicant the Colonel so

skillfully prepared, he grew more and more confidential. "I don't mind tellin' you," he said, "that I'm a candidate for a Fed'ral office. Now, if I am a Colonel, wouldn't that hurt me?"

Colonel Dunklin looked at Colonel Bollinger and smiled. Colonel Bollinger carelessly threw a piece of lemon peal into the cuspidor and said, with dignity:

"The fact that a man is a Colonel is good and sufficient reason why he is eligible for any office whatsoever, *per se*. And if the office does not seek him, he is perfectly justified in seeking the office. And I hold that if the public service appears so to require, he is free at any time to change his political views. In accordance with an ancient and honorable precedent, if he is not a candidate for office, he may drink socially with one who is, but he is not to be subsidized, hampered or impeded by such courtesy. For example — George, bring in three more of the same kind, and just a dash of Angostura."

Tubbs's hand went down into his pocket, but the Colonel waved him off with a gesture full of imperious eloquence.

"No, sir, not in Mizzoora. You are my guest, sir, and shall pay for nothing in my presence. George, you will see that the gentleman has whatever he wishes, and that he wants for nothing."

George grinned, and Tubbs felt another weight added to the burden of his obligation.

"And now, sir," says Colonel Bollinger, rising, "I must bid you good day. I hope to see you often in Mizzoora, sir, and to welcome you to the extent of our poor hospitality."

Colonel Dunklin likewise stood up and looked at Tubbs with his melancholy eyes. And both the Colonels bowed with great elegance and dignity, and shook Tubbs's hand and promised themselves the honor of his society at an early day. And as they passed out Tubbs could hear Colonel Bollinger's sonorous voice discoursing on the fineness of the day and the glorious outlook for the mint crop.

"After all," soliloquized Tubbs, as he leaned back in his chair and gave himself up to pleasant reflections, "I sometimes wonder if we ain't too hard on these Missourians. Of course they're dead wrong, perlitically, and they're all off on the great principles of prohibition. But they're genial and friendly, and I ain't got a word to say agin their hospitality. That whitefish was prime and the liquors fust-class." And Tubbs closed his eyes in an ecstasy of recollection.

From this agreeable reverie he was roused by the arrival of George, who respectfully laid a slip of paper before him. Tubbs picked it up with a slight sinking in the pit of his stomach and read:

"Whitefish, 60 cents; cigars, 50 cents; drinks, $2.10. Total, $3.20. What's this?"

"De bill."

"But I don't owe no bill. This is Colonel Bollinger's matter. You heard what he said."

The negro grinned. "I reckon de Kunnel done fergit. De Kunnel mighty cur'us dat way. He fergit a heap o' times, when de odder gen'men have to pay."

Tubbs bowed his head for a full minute. When he raised his face it shone with a new light and was glorified by wisdom.

"George," said he, "take a good look at me. I am from Kansas, and my name is Tubbs. If ever you see me walkin' into this robbers' roost with a Colonel anybody from Missouri, I want you to kick me down to the river and into it. Here's your three twenty."

An hour later Tubbs stood on the bluff that looks far over into Kansas. In front of him was the clear sky, and the fresh air, suggestive of sobriety and virtue; behind him the smoke and dirt of the city, typifying deceit and fraud and injured innocence. As he climbed into a cable car to bear him across the river, another car came up the hill, and a familiar voice cried out:

"Going home, are you? A pleasant journey to you. Come and see me when you revisit the city."

Tubbs looked at Colonel Bollinger, who was

waving a cordial farewell from the retreating car, and almost fell from the grip in his astonishment and wrath.

"Well, I am "—

But whatever he was, was lost in the clang of the gripman's bell.

The Deaf Ear.

THE DEAF EAR.

Mr. Littlejohn Jenks, in spite of many hours of research and patient inquiry in the various departments of his family connection, was never quite able to discover at what time or in what way he acquired a deaf ear. The traditions of the household did not point to scarlet fever or measles; as a boy he was not allowed to go to the swimming-hole, that enemy of the organ of hearing, and he was not even able to recall that the family methods of punishment, while very ingenious and numerous and altogether painful, and extending over a large area of epidermis, included that resounding salute on the side of the head which is so undeservedly popular with thoughtless parents. So Mr. Jenks, admitting the unimpeachable fact of his hardness of hearing, had all the evidence in the world to prove that the affliction was in defiance of human precedent and contrary to physical laws. From the moment that young Littlejohn emerged from the nursery he was made to feel that he had been hatched out of the duck egg. A blithe, joyous lad, he was fond of his companions and of his sports, but his was unhappily a confidence that was ill-repaid by his playmates, who took full advantage of his good nature and his infirmity. He recalled in after life the memorable day when old Spanker took charge of the district school, and by his marvelous instinct detected the boys in a flagrant outrage on scholastic propriety.

"Who did this?" queried old Spanker.

"Littlejohn Jenks," replied the boys, softly.

"Did you do this, Jenks?"

Now Littlejohn had not heard a word of the conversation, but a scheming little boy close at hand whispered promptingly:

"Wants to know if yer sorry."

"Oh, yes, sir, if you please, sir," replied Littlejohn, smartly.

Thereupon old Spanker fell upon him with an awful grip and a terrifying strap, and larruped him up and down the row of benches, balancing to the right and swinging to the left until the dignity of the school-room had been fully maintained and vindicated. It is due to old Spanker to say that when the facts in the case were developed he made a handsome apology, which Littlejohn did not hear, but which was repeated to him many years after by one of his schoolmates on the gladsome occasion of old Spanker's funeral.

Such incidents as this soon gave Littlejohn a reserve and a caution beyond his years. His buoyancy and confidence were replaced by timidity and suspicion. He avoided his comrades and shrank from his teachers, and as for the girls, he was on speaking terms with few and on hearing terms with none. He went through college very much as a blind man would go through an art gallery, and graduated just in time to receive the blessing of his departing parents (interpreted to him after the funeral), and to come into possession of an income large enough to discourage any improper appetite for labor.

As Mr. Littlejohn Jenks increased in years and experience he decreased in hearing and confidence. While his money and his gentle birth gave to him an unquestioned standing in society, he was slow to take advantage of its privileges, and slower still to trust to the integrity of the encouraging smiles that were not infrequently lavished upon him by the mothers of marriageable young women. From time to time he cherished the delusive hope that his infirmity might be cured, and occasionally he fell into the hands of specialists, who ran long rods up his nostrils and into his ears, and gouged his palate, and applied burning and torturesome chemicals thereto, until what little nerve he had was entirely dissipated. But, beyond the recollection of many hours of agony and the receipt of a large and comprehensive bill, there were no notable results. So Mr. Jenks at last abandoned hope and treatment and gave himself up to his fate.

That a gentleman of Mr. Jenks's means and personality, whose greatest charm was a most alluring air of settled melancholy, should be allowed to escape entirely the demands of society, was not to be entertained. At times he yielded weakly to the efforts made for his ensnaring, and those concessions were always the bitterest recollections of his life. It was his misfortune to patronize a dining over which the Reverend Mr. Pentateuch was requested to say grace. Perhaps from his connection with the English church, Mr. Pentateuch was accustomed to divide his blessings, as it were, into first and second lessons. Be this as it may, Mr. Jenks, in his anxiety to appear thoroughly at his ease, noticed a half-smile on the pretty face of his *vis-à-vis*, and reciprocated with a look of such innocent ardor that the young woman was thrown into blushing confusion. Just at this time Mr. Pentateuch, having paused in deference to his long established custom, was proceeding with the formula which trusts that "these viands may be sanctified to our use," when, to the unspeakable horror of the company, Mr. Jenks addressed the young woman with the untimely and not altogether original observation, "A penny for your thoughts." The indignation of the clergyman and the pain of the hostess only added to the mirth of the guests, and the rest of the grace was intelligible to the Deity alone.

It was also Mr. Jenks's misfortune to be seated invariably next to the visiting young lady, who was unaware of his infirmity, and this led to many unhappy results. As long as Mr. Jenks could do the talking he was reasonably safe, for his conversation dealt exclusively with assertion that involved no argument, and never trenched on the province of the interrogatory. But Mr. Jenks was not a gentleman of fluent speech or surging ideas, and it always happened that, despite his most arduous endeavors, the monologue soon languished. As has been related, Mr. Jenks's engaging air of melancholy often won for him the confidence of the ladies, and perhaps this is why Miss Alsopp, who was placed contiguous to the deaf ear, felt irresistibly impelled to communicate to him the harrowing tale of her aunt, who had lost her life in a burning vessel at sea.

"And it is related by Doctor Penfield, one of the survivors," went on Miss Alsopp, "that during that dreadful scene my aunt did not lose her equanimity. Just before she was enveloped by the flames she cried out with a loud voice, like the martyred Stephen, and went to her rest singing one of the sweet songs of the Christian faith."

Mr. Jenks had heard nothing of this heart-rending story, but he gathered from the smiles of his

9

neighbor on the right, who was rallying her partner, that the tale had been a sprightly one. So he leaned back and laughed heartily, and said: "Good, good, very neat!" The look of horror on Miss Alsopp's face soon gave way to indignation. She whispered to her neighbor, and in an unduly short time it had spread around the table that Jenks was uproariously drunk. Not until Mr. Jenks was putting on his overcoat in the dressing-room did he learn the particulars of his error, and by that time the offended lady had demanded the protection of a loathsome rival and disappeared.

This episode so weighed on Mr. Jenks's spirits that never thereafter was he known to smile in society. As he confessed in his diary, he took no chances. In vain the company joined in a general burst, in vain the brightest sallies were thrown at him *fortissimo*. "It won't do," he said, with a sad shake of the head; "you see, by the time I catch the joke and laugh, the company may be talking about religion or death, and I'm sure to get the worst end of it. It's much better to wait and do all my laughing at home." Which showed that Jenks possessed the kindest heart and tenderest sensibilities.

Mr. Jenks's besetting weakness was music. It was considered quite a *bon mot* to ask Jenks if he was going to see the concert. Not content with patronizing all the celebrities of the day, Mr. Jenks studied the flute and violin, and sometimes yielded to a polite request to play in company. These exhibitions were purely experimental, for Mr. Jenks was at constant warfare with his accompanist, both as to time and pitch, and produced the most extraordinary effects in his efforts to harmonize instruments a quarter of a tone apart. But as the company never paid the slightest attention to Jenks's performance, except occasionally to execrate it, and went on with its conversation, perfectly satisfied that the breach of etiquette would be lost on the performer, no serious consequences resulted.

So the years went by, and Mr. Jenks began to experience that unsettled feeling, that indefinable longing and loneliness that come with protracted bachelorhood. His companions had married and prospered, as far as prosperity can come with marriage. He had officiated as attendant at weddings and as godfather at christenings, until a genuine rivalry had sprung up between him and his rector.

"We esteem you highly in the parish, my dear Jenks," said the Reverend Mr. Surplice; "your conduct is generally exemplary. But by this life of singleness you deprive a girl of a worthy husband, you neglect one of God's ordinances, and you — ahem — you rob me of what ought to be a substantial fee."

This clerical reproof set Mr. Jenks to thinking. He confessed his loneliness and willingness to embrace matrimony on favorable terms. He admitted that, while he scouted the idea so frequently advanced, that two can live as cheaply as one, two loving hearts can spend money more profitably than one. But where should he apply? He ran over the list of eligible young women of his acquaintance, and sighed to think that the lot had been carefully sorted and robbed of its chief ornaments. No, stop! Agatha Brown remained. He had known Agatha since she was a little blue-eyed, waxen-cheeked maiden in pinafores. He had followed her with regular remembrances up through the candy, peanut, doll stages, beyond the valentine period, even to the Easter flower epoch. He had noticed that Agatha was always considerate, that she never laughed at his blunders, and, come to think of it, he had observed lately a disposition on her part to blush and tremble in his presence. The more vividly he recalled those blushes the more firmly was he convinced that Agatha was created for him and he for Agatha. Upon these hints, like the swarthy gentleman in the play, he spoke.

"I have brought myself to believe, my dear Agatha," said Mr. Jenks, as they sat in the little parlor, from which, with rare instinct and acumen, the parents had withdrawn, "that in your heart lurks some pity for my lonely life. I feel, as does every man in this trying moment, that, with my natural handicap and my lack of graces. I am unworthy the affection of a good and pure woman. But at least I am a man of means and am free from all large and contaminating vices. I love you, and I have taken this opportunity of asking you to share my lot and monopolize my time and my affections."

Pending this speech the gentle Agatha blushed and trembled more violently than usual, and at its close the tears that rose to her blue eyes gave them the appearance of violets in a shower. But, like a good and pure woman, she regained her composure with marvelous celerity.

"I will not disguise from you, dear Littlejohn," she answered, "that while I have never looked upon you as a future husband, I have always been sensible of your goodness, and have envied her who might gain the wealth of your affections. And for this reason I give myself to you with all hope and confidence. How I shall endeavor to prove worthy of your great love you may trust in time to know." So saying, she modestly turned away her head and cast down her eyes.

Now Mr. Jenks, recognizing too late that he had unfortunately placed Agatha in juxtaposition to his bad ear, was striving by every means to shift his location and to comprehend her reply. But, despite his most tactical efforts, he was able to catch only the last word, "know," which, through the criminally perverse orthoepy of the English language, he construed into a negative, an impression greatly heightened by the young woman's perceptible air of pity and regret. Mr. Jenks was a man of pride, and, stunned as he was, it was only for a moment. He burst into a cheery laugh, and said, with affected jocularity:

"Don't be downcast, Agatha. I was only joking. It's a little way I have. It's all right, even if you don't love me."

Poor Agatha was in despair. "You — you don't understand," she gasped, and then she stood on her toes and screamed "I love you," until it seemed as if the entire neighborhood must be cognizant of the fact.

"That's all right — all right," replied Mr. Jenks; "I don't blame you a bit. And the more I think it over the more ridiculous the matter strikes me."

Mr. Jenks by this time was in the hall, putting on his overcoat, while Agatha, struggling with baffled love and tears and rage, was close behind, reiterating her affection with maidenly saving clauses.

"Good night, Agatha," said Mr. Jenks, magnanimously; "forget our little joke and be a sister to me."

Twenty-four hours later the blue-eyed maiden, in pique and desperation, accepted a proposition from a commercial traveler for a grocery house, and after the wedding bells had pealed Mr. Jenks heard, with throbs of anguish, the true story of his luckless courtship.

Time soothes all griefs, and Mr. Jenks, albeit he had withdrawn from society and its empty pleasures, became reconciled to the mysterious ways of Providence. The gentle Agatha, at the suggestion of her husband and in deference to his family name and pride, had presented to the commercial traveler two little images of herself, and as Mr. Jenks saw them playing with their dolls and running to meet their worthy but unsentimental sire, his heart was stirred by strange emotions. "Shall I," he reasoned to himself, "because of one bitter and terrible mistake, longer endure this wretched and monotonous existence? Shall I not show this presumptuous drummer that I too have paternal instincts, which may be gratified by the cultivation of a respectful attachment and by the exercise of a little patience?"

The object of Mr. Jenks's second endeavor was a vivacious young lady, in temperament and charms very unlike the blue-eyed Agatha. Not disinclined to flirt, and seeing in Mr. Jenks a suitable mark for her seductive batteries, she led him on by feminine arts until one evening, strolling sentimentally along the river bank, he repeated to her the formula which five years before he had tried with such embarrassing results. Notwithstanding her merry words. Miss Daisy — she was a true Missouri girl — had a kind heart, and was visibly affected by Mr. Jenks's earnestness. Her agitation increased as she reflected on the consequences of her levity, and, although she assured Mr. Jenks that she "could never, never be his wife," a sympathetic tear of remorse stole down her cheek. According to usage, Mr. Jenks did not succeed in catching a word of the pronunciamento of rejection, but, remembering his former error and seeing her tears and confusion, caught her to his breast and imprinted passionate kisses on her hair and cheek and mouth, wherever they chanced to fall. The frightened girl screamed lustily, and a policeman rushing up, and spying a struggling maid in the arms of a desperate villain, brought Mr. Jenks to the ground by a few well-directed blows from his *insigne* of office. For ten minutes there was a commingling of hysterics and explanations and official skepticism, but at last, the young lady interceding, Mr. Jenks was allowed to depart, and the heroine was escorted to her home under police protection.

This second *contretemps* was too much for Mr. Jenks's nerves. He withdrew permanently from society, engaged a housekeeper of austere visage and impregnable and unquestioned morality, and gave himself up to the cultivation of flowers and the gentle arts. Late at night the youths and maidens, returning from their evening pleasure, could hear the melancholy notes of his flute or the sad strains of his violin, and why they crossed the street at that particular point was always charitably suppressed. But Mr. Jenks's life was not the less worthy and beautiful because he was deprived, in so sorrowful a measure, of one of the most agreeable senses. He delighted in good works, helped the poor and the needy, comforted the afflicted, and cheerfully accepted all the sponsorial responsibilities which were thrust upon him, and they were many. He was "uncle" to half the children in the town, and at Christmas time the most extraordinary boxes and mysterious packages were smuggled in and out of the house, while Mr. Jenks could be observed running to and fro in a state of nervous excitement.

As his hair whitened and the furrows showed more plainly in his face, Mr. Jenks's responsibilities, *ex officio*, increased. Agatha's two little girls had grown up and had two or more little girls of their own, and over them the deaf old gentleman, with capacious pockets in which confections and oranges always lurked, exercised the privileged sway of "grandfather." And it was a happy sight to see the old man followed by a troop of laughing children, pretending to be angry with them for "making so much noise," and slily slipping bonbons into their hands and dropping peanuts and almonds out of his pocket that they might excite a scramble and more noise.

At last Mr. Jenks succumbed to the ravages of time, and took to his bed. Disease made rapid inroads on his enfeebled constitution, and it was mournfully whispered about town that "old Jenks had to go." In this emergency the new minister perceived his duty, and went to the old man's bedside to administer those consolations that are the rightful property of the church. As he took his station at the left of the bed, Mr. Jenks, failing to catch the features of his visitor, conceived him to be one of the physicians, for whom, as a class, he had the most profound contempt. The new minister was saying:

"In this hour of travail, my departing friend, I may hope that you have learned to rely on the glorious promises of the Word, and that from the precious book you have been drawn to the Great Physician, who healeth all our infirmities and maketh us well."

"Makes what well?" snapped Mr. Jenks, who had caught only the concluding words. "I took the blamed stuff three times yesterday, and I'm worse to-day." And he turned his face to the wall, requesting the nurse to show the man out. But the new minister, however shocked by the apparent wickedness of the dying man, lingered on the threshold and offered up a fervent petition for the pardon and conversion of the blaspheming infidel.

And now occurred a most singular and impressive phenomenon. When the doctor came and looked at the patient with his experienced eye, he said: "He will live three hours." At the end of that time there was apparently no change. An imprudent friend, putting himself in communication with the good ear, related what the physician had predicted, and congratulated him on the hopeful nature of his symptoms in weathering the crisis. Mr. Jenks made no reply, but turned over and quietly passed away. In an able essay, read before the medical society, the physician contended that the prolongation of Mr. Jenks's life was due entirely to a misunderstanding; that he had stood near the patient's deaf ear when he made the diagnosis and the prediction, and that to this circumstance only must be attributed the temporary failure of medical science and the reversal of medical precedent. Therefore he maintained that a deaf ear, while not an infallible preventive of death, is often a helpful factor in prolonging human life, and is a fit subject for the most careful and exhaustive experiments when the patient is apparently *in articulo mortis*. This essay created a great sensation in medical circles. Scientific journals took it up, foreign academies discussed it, and the International Society of Physicians and Surgeons sent a complimentary letter to the writer thanking him for his efforts and his discovery in the field of science.

As Mr. Jenks's friends gathered around his bier and looked upon his peaceful face, it was suggested, not irreverently but with real solicitude, that his right ear should be a little elevated, that when Gabriel blew the trump the other inhabitants of the churchyard might not have an unfair advantage. And when all the others had gone out, Agatha, now a widow and a grandmother, with little white curls that peeped out of her cap, and with eyes that still retained their violet blue, lingered a moment, just long enough to give one fond look and to whisper, "I love you," as she had said it many years before.

The new minister, still smarting under a recollection of the blasphemous scene in the sick-chamber, delivered a powerful address on the uncertainty of life and the necessity of preparation. But when the coffin was lowered into the grave the mothers led the children a little nearer, and with their infant hands they heaped roses and forget-me-nots and immortelles upon the casket, the tributes of three generations to the old friend. And what they said of the dead he living could not have heard without a protesting blush. And how they spoke of him and praised him in their homes that night must have warmed that deaf ear as it lay so cold and still beneath the flowers.

The Confession of a Crime.

THE CONFESSION OF A CRIME.

Down in one of the central counties of Missouri, in the heart of the great corn-belt, pretty Lucy Howard was "raised." That she certainly was "raised" is not to be disputed, for she is authority for the expression, and can, if necessary, bring up a formidable array of kinfolk and neighbors to prove the assertion. Lucy's father lived in one of the older towns of this section of Missouri, which, for one reason or another, has escaped the immigration and other contaminating influences which, in a measure, have afflicted the border counties. Therefore society, despite the ravages of war, is in a settled and placid state, and resembles more closely the better condition of things in the old South. Here the Missourian attains his greatest courtliness, and life is characterized by the warmest hospitality. And here the girls, rounded and rosy-cheeked, develop into the most beautiful womanhood, with all the charms and graces and soft speech of the Southern clime.

Colonel Howard was a Southerner by birth, in association and in every instinct. He had been a fire-eater, a rebel and a Democrat since early manhood, and he was proud of it. He was also inclined to indolence, the result of paternal inheritance, and he was not ashamed of that, for your true old-school Missouri gentleman has fixed and stern ideas concerning the elevating quality of labor. "This constant digging and delving," said the Colonel, in one of his many leisure moments; "this perpetual striving after money or rushing after a temporary gain, makes us a nation of dyspeptic Yankees and destroys all the finer and nobler impulses of an old and tranquil civilization."

Lucy, naturally, grew up under languorous conditions, which, however, took nothing from her beauty or her amiability and gentleness of character. Perhaps the stern tenets of the Christian, or Campbellite, Church, to which her family was attached, had left an impress on her mind in its formative period, and had given her that stern conscientiousness which so marked her rule of life. In early girlhood she had gone to a sectarian college, where the girls wore ridiculous uniforms and praised the Lord two or three times a day for the pious work of Alexander Campbell, and never conversed with a man, save on an occasional Saturday night, under the most distressing conditions.

But nothing could mar Lucy's beauty or destroy the contentment of her disposition. And when, every Sunday morning, her sweet face peeped out under the college sun-bonnet, and her beautiful voice rose above all others in the choir chamber, the reason of the great outpouring of the young men was clear. For everybody in the sanctuary turned to look at Lucy, and all the young fellows sighed for her day of graduation. Robert Callaway said not a word, for he had taken advantage of the summer vacation to gather Lucy unto himself, and like two orderly and well-conducted young people they reveled discreetly in their promises of love, and bided their time.

So Robert went off to the city to guide and instruct the masses from the noble standpoint of a journalist. And Lucy retired to her father's house and bloomed with the roses in the summer and the hyacinths in the winter, and cultivated and exercised her glorious voice until all the mocking-birds were distracted with vexation and envy. And she waited very patiently for Robert, and calmly rebuked numerous presumptuous admirers for impertinent offers of marriage. And Robert wrote regularly and cheerfully from the city, and one day the bird sang in her heart with an unusual caroling, for Robert telegraphed that he had obtained a "scoop" on his loathsome contemporary, and was in high favor with the gentleman whose most painful duty it was, occasionally, to raise salaries.

But an end comes to all periods of waiting, and

one fine night in late October the Colonel's old house was lighted up from cellar to garret, and friends and neighbors poured into the great parlor, while the darkies were rushing about in excitement, savory smells issued from the kitchen, and the popping of corks was heard in the second story back. And in front of the piano stood Lucy, looking like a Vestal virgin in her robe of white, with a flush on her cheeks, and just the faintest twitching of her pretty mouth, and tears of moisture in her blue eyes. And she was telling Robert, who clasped her hand, something that has been told many times before and will continue to be told long after these generations have passed away.

Back they went to the city, and Robert, who was now on confidential and easy terms with that great man, the cashier of the *Independent,* fitted up a comfortable home which bespoke much love and happiness. And in the main they lived like turtle-doves, with those occasional honest differences of opinion which afflict all good married folk. For Robert's journalistic training had led him into devious ways, and had bestowed upon him a proud and haughty mind, so that, when Lucy would gently prod him as to his religious duties on the holy Sabbath morn, he would occasionally rebel and flippantly remark that he had "forgotten more than Aleck Campbell ever knew." Whereat the great tears would well up into Lucy's eyes, and in the end Robert, who had a kind heart, would be a heavy financial sufferer by reason of his irreverence. And at times the domestic would take unto herself the wings of the morning, and Lucy would be compelled to go into the kitchen. These were the sun-spots of their married life, for when Lucy did not forget to put the baking-powder in the biscuits, she committed other and more serious indiscretions, with the result that her meals, as Robert genially expressed it, partook of the nature of burnt offerings, as became a Christian household. But with all their petty trials, they lived very happily, and the increased breadth and vigor of the tone of the *Independent* bore witness to Robert's enlarged scope.

Toward the end of the first year of their married life, Robert, having been gently reminded by the pious Lucy that it was Wednesday evening, suddenly remembered that he had a most pressing engagement at the office, one that under no circumstances would admit even an hour's postponement. The gentle girl sighed as he reached for his hat and cane, and believed him implicitly when he kissed her and, in respectful language, cursed the claims of business that took him away from the hour of prayer. But after he had gone, and she had heard him madly whistling and shouting as he dashed for a down-town car, she went to the piano and sang a few holy songs to put her mind in a calm and religiously receptive state. Then she called next door for her neighbor and old girl friend, Mrs. Boone, whose husband had likewise been mysteriously summoned to the office, and together those two exemplary women journeyed to the house of worship.

Now it chanced that evening that the Rev. Dr. Moniteau delivered his first discourse of a series of lectures on the duties of wives. Having buried three, this excellent man was abundantly able to grasp his subject intelligently and to present it with forcefulness. "I ask you, my dear sisters," he said:—he started to say brothers and sisters, but caught himself, as there were no brothers present—"I ask you if you have been true to your husbands in thought as well as deed. Have you given to them the confidence and the love that should exist at all times between husband and wife? I think that perhaps I may see before me at this moment a wife who has been derelict in this precious duty. Perhaps she is young and impulsive and thoughtless, and thinks that her little sins of omission and commission are too trifling to be told to the man whom she has vowed to love, honor and obey. Ah, my dear sisters, do not fall into this grievous error. Remember that you may have no secrets from your husband. Remember that he is entitled to know your innermost heart. If there rests in your mind to-night, sister, any little error, however trifling, you may have withheld from him, go to him, throw yourself upon his breast and say: 'My husband, I come to you in love and confidence like a little child to its father. I have kept back from you a fault. Let me tell it and know that it is not treasured up against me.' And trust, dear sister, to his great affection and forgiving love."

Poor Lucy occupied a seat directly in front of the speaker. It had happened in his godless days, before the light shined round about him, journeying, as it were, to Damascus, that the Rev. Dr. Moniteau had acquired a glass eye. This eye rested on Lucy with such fixed and awful intensity that she fell all of a tremble, and her little heart thumped against her ribs with the anguish of an unpunctured felon. And at that moment the ghost of an unexpected crime rose up before her, and the thought was so horrible that she almost screamed out in meeting, and so dreadful was the remembrance that she was entirely unable to join in the congregational singing which the Rev. Dr. Moniteau led in particularly strident tones.

As they walked home together Lucy said, timidly:

"Gertrude, what do you think of Dr. Moniteau's advice?"

"Think?" snapped Mrs. Boone. "I think it's all bosh. That's what I think."

"But, Gertrude," interposed Lucy, "oughtn't we to tell our husbands everything?"

Mrs. Boone wheeled around. "Now look here, Lucy Callaway, don't you make any mistakes in the first year of your married life. Do you suppose your husband tells you all his escapades? Do you suppose I'm going to sit up every night for a month while John Boone goes over the story of his ante-nuptial misdeeds — granting that he'd be fool enough to tell me? When he reeled off that clumsy story about an 'engagement' to-night, didn't I know that it was merely an excuse to get out of going to prayer-meeting? I shall tell him so too, to-morrow, but not to-night, for that would spoil both our evenings."

"I can't answer for Mr. Boone," said Lucy, decisively, "but Robbie would never deceive me."

Mrs. Boone looked at the girl compassionately. "You're a good girl, Lucy," she said; "I don't know a better. But take my advice and don't make a fool of yourself."

"Nevertheless," answered Lucy, firmly, as the ghost rose up again, "I shall examine my heart to-night, and if I find any secret there I shall tell Robbie at once."

However, when Robert came home and reported the cares and vexations of the office with more than his customary fervor, Lucy's courage failed her. After all, it would be much better to make the confession in the morning, when her nerves were more composed and when her husband, refreshed by slumber, would be in better condition to bear up under the revelation. But in the morning the conditions were even more unfavorable. Breakfast was late and Robert was querulous. Plainly it was no time to precipitate a crisis, and the gentle Lucy confessed a feeling of relief when her husband left the house and a stay of execution was granted.

In the evening a social dissipation at a neighbor's interfered. The next day Robert went out of town on business, and so the matter ran along for a week. When Wednesday night came around Robert was caught napping. He had arranged with a friend at the office to call for him in great haste a little after seven o'clock; but the friend had overlooked the appointment, and, as no reasonable excuse presented, Robert put on the best face possible and went to Doctor Moniteau's second lecture. The Doctor emphasized his previous address, and his glass eye caught Lucy early in the action, and held her fast. The ordeal was even more trying than the first awakening of conscience. And to add to the discomfort of the poor girl Robert said, with affected solemnity, before they went to bed that night: "Lucy, I hope you will profit by Brother Moniteau's observations. Remember that a wife should have no secrets from her husband. Repent and confess before it is too late."

The days that followed were like torture to the young wife. A dozen times she was on the point of throwing herself on Robert's manly breast, but something invariably came up to thwart her. In the afternoon, while Robert was down town, she would have a sort of rehearsal, the pillow on the sofa representing Robbie. But the pillow was so obdurate, its wrath so terrible, and its invective so relentless, that Lucy was completely annihilated, and when her husband came home she was glad enough to keep up her life of deception, and to welcome the living presence in place of its inanimate avenger.

At the third lecture the malevolence, the terrors, the offended majesty of the glass eye were simply beyond endurance. It burned into Lucy's soul and seemed to leave a deep opening through which all might see her wicked heart. She bowed her head in the pew and wept scalding tears of shame and remorse. And when she left the sanctuary her mind was fully made up: she would confess — the next day.

When morning came she was much comforted to find that her resolution was unshaken. "But," the devil whispered to her, "there is no sense in doing this thing hastily and blunderingly. Tact is a woman's best weapon. It is all right to confess, but proper means of preservation and defense are always allowable." So Lucy allowed Robert to escape, and fixed that evening for the revelation that might make her a widow or a corpse.

All day long, in conjunction with the devil, she made her preparations to mitigate the horrors of the evening. She put deft little artistic touches all over the house, placed the new center-piece on the dining-room table, and filled the flower-jar with roses. Then she tied up a bunch of pansies with a love-knot and laid them near Robert's plate, for Robert was very partial to pansies. And she went into the kitchen and superintended and accomplished marvels of cookery: spring chicken fried to a turn, with rich cream gravy; such beaten biscuits as were never before seen in the city; luscious corn-bread that she had heard him say his mother used to make; the freshest and best vegetables in the market; a strawberry short-cake that was simply incomparable, and coffee that gave out a delicious perfume a block away. And she even took ten cents from her private funds and bought him a nice cigar at the grocery, the groceryman assuring her that it was good enough for the President. And at five o'clock she went to her room and put on her red China silk, which Robert admired so much, and which, cut low around the neck, showed off her beautiful throat and revealed her exquisite arms. And she hung around her neck the gold chain and heart which Robert had given her when they were lovers in the old Missouri town. And, all preparations being completed, she plumped down on her knees and asked God to give her strength for her task.

When Robert came home he was visibly moved by the evidences of wifeliness. He complimented the appearance of the house, admired the roses, and pinned the pansies on his coat. As for the dinner, he vowed it was a dream, and when he had finished his second piece of shortcake he went over and took Lucy's face in his hands and kissed her, and said, feelingly:

"My dear little wife, how pretty you are to-night!"

And Lucy turned away that he might not notice the tears that rose to her eyes, while he took advantage of the moment to slip the President's cigar into his coat-tail pocket and to substitute one of his own in its stead.

They went into the library, and Robert, being in that boastful stage that comes to a man after a hearty dinner, complacently read to his wife the proof-sheets of his great article on the influence of archæologic research among the Zunis. And although Lucy constantly labored under the impression that Zunis were in some way connected with Doctor Kane and Sir John Franklin, she listened with devouring interest, and kissed him whenever he looked as if he had made a particularly good point. And as he looked that way particularly often she was more or less constantly employed. Then she sat down at the piano and sang all her prettiest songs, as only she could sing them; songs of love and broken hearts and little barks on the ocean and little birds in the nests, and a hundred other things connected with the idealities of a perfectly lovely existence. And Robert leaned back in his big arm-chair, and looked so happy and so contented that Lucy said to herself, in the extremity of her grief: "I can't tell him now! I can't tell him now!"

At last Robert said: "Let's call it a day," which was his customary way of announcing that it was bedtime. So he departed to his chamber, whistling a merry air that showed his heart was light and his conscience free. But Lucy remained behind with her secret and her sorrow, and wrestled with herself, for she knew the hour of confession was at hand. And presently Robert returned, for he had forgotten to look after the back windows, put out the gas in the dining-room, wind the clock and perform other functions which the Zunis fortunately escaped. He was in his night-robe.

Now a man in his robe of night is not a pleasing spectacle. The artistic world is a unit on that point. Lucy, whose temperament was entirely artistic, had often deplored the conventionality of fashion that shortens a gentleman's sleeping-garment to a degree bordering on the scandalous, and had often threatened to ornament Robert's gowns with tucks and frills and other purely feminine accessories. But this night she was occupied with her grief to the exclusion of all inartistic views. She only thought: "How noble, how manly he looks! How can I bring myself to forfeit my darling's love!" And Robert was meanwhile stubbing his toe on the stairs and writhing with pain and an explosion of unprintable language, utterly unconscious of these tributes to his manliness, his nobility and his qualifications as a darling.

It had been Lucy's intention to follow as literally as possible the excellent instructions of the Rev. Dr. Moniteau. But her preparations were so exhaustive, and her second and final petition for sustaining strength was so protracted, that Robert had traveled at least two-thirds of the distance to the land of unconsciousness before she could bring herself to the point of claiming his attention. And even then she was embarrassed by the discovery that it would be impossible to throw herself on his breast as she had contemplated, for he was reposing with his face on the outer edge of the bed, rendering such proceeding not only ridiculous but impracticable. She found also, to her horror, that in her agitation she had entirely for-

gotten the ministerial formula, and was compelled
to fall back on her own resources to bear her over
the crisis. She nerved herself, shut her eyes and
said:

"Robbie!"

A stifled grunt gave the assurance that Robert
was, in a measure, awake to the importance of the
occasion.

"Robbie, I've been wanting to tell you something for a long, long time. It has been on my mind constantly, but we have been so happy together that I couldn't bring myself to tell you. I knew I was doing wrong, but I didn't know how wicked and deceitful it was until I heard Doctor Moniteau's lecture on the duties of a wife. And, Robbie, you know you told me yourself that a wife should have no secrets from her husband, so, if I am going to give you pain, dear, it is partly because I am obeying your command. You have always said that it made you happy to think that you were my first sweetheart—and you were. Robbie, indeed you were. I never cared for any man but you, and I know I should never have married anybody if I had never met you. But of course I couldn't help it if some of the boys liked me, and, really, Robbie, it wasn't my fault because Tom Cooper kept tagging after me and pestering me with his silliness. And one night—this was long, long before I met you, Robbie—he was taking me

home, and he—he kissed me. I know it was
perfectly dreadful, Robbie, and I was very angry
and hurt at the time. I wanted to tell you about
it when we first became engaged, but I didn't dare.
And then we were married, and it was harder than
ever. And I suppose I should have taken it on
my conscience down to the grave if it hadn't been
for you and Doctor Moniteau. It isn't too late,
Robbie, is it?"

A dreadful silence followed the disclosure. Lucy
felt her heart beating wildly, and her brain
throbbed with mad and awful fancies. She saw
herself standing in the divorce court, telling the
story of her shame to an unpitying judge and a
crowd of vulgar and jeering spectators. And
Robbie sat near with sternly averted face, and her
old father and mother were bowing their heads in
humiliation and anguish.

"You ain't mad, are you, Robbie?"

Again that ominous silence. But Lucy thought
she heard a faint movement of the pillow, and the
terrible story of Othello and Desdemona rushed
into her mind. What if this gentle Robbie were
indeed a fiend incarnate when his jealous passions
were aroused? What if in his disappointment
and rage and wounded love he should rise up and
strangle her or smother her dying cries under the
soft repository of goose-feathers! Lucy was chilled
with fright. Her impulse was to slip out of bed

and steal to a place of safety. But what would she gain? Life? Was life without Robbie preferable to death? Was death more to be dreaded than that awful scene in the court-room and countless years of biting remorse? No! If her crime merited death it would be sweet to die by Robbie's hand. And she closed her eyes again and endeavored to recall a little prayer for the dying which she had seen in a prayer-book, and which had made a marked impression on her mind.

But still that fearful, agonizing silence. It was beginning to be too much for Lucy's nervous system. Such misery the victim experiences when he is strapped upon the bascule of the guillotine, waiting for the knife to fall. The moonlight struggled in through the slanting blinds and disclosed the injured husband lying on his side, his left arm under his head, his right carelessly resting on the spread. Lucy raised herself, and, leaning on her elbow, peered into his face.

The brute was fast asleep.

The Old Major's Story.

THE OLD MAJOR'S STORY.

It was down in the Current River country, and at that period of development this was not a country to conjure by. The villages were small, ragged and depressing, with apparently no excuse for being, save to break up the monotony of travel on the railway lying between Springfield and Memphis. We had ridden across a dreary waste of miles from the fishing-grounds in a conveyance the atrocious discomfort of which baffled all comparisons, and had missed the train as a finishing touch of misery. It needed only this to round off an excursion of pleasure that had been prolific of everything except pleasure. The fish, if fish there were, had refused to bite, but this deficiency had been supplied by a large variety of insects, which had welcomed us in a hospitable manner. We had feasted on bacon and hominy, hominy and bacon, until we had entirely forgotten the taste of all other articles of food, and looked upon them as a sort of tormenting dream. And the highwayman, as we called him, who had all the external signs of a Bald-Knobber, and all the natural outcroppings of a bandit, and who had consented to convey us to the train, had stipulated for a consideration so ruinous that the pool was barely able to meet his demands. At the same time it was deemed politic to submit without a murmur. It is astonishing how a few rocks and woods and ravines will make cowards of brave men.

Four of us were in the party — the General Passenger and Ticket Agent, who organized it, a middle-aged lawyer with a good practice, a young doctor with no practice, and the wretched author of the tale. It was not at this crisis an agreeable party, one that would shed luster on the civilization of the nineteenth century. We were tired and hungry and cross, and, at the same time, wet and dry, a paradox that every fisherman readily understands and appreciates. The engine of our train had slipped an eccentric forty miles down the road, and was bulletined for four o'clock in the morning. The small hotel was a ghastly picture of misery, and seemed so full of terrors and unknown horrors that nobody dared go to bed, although it was then nine o'clock, promising a long sleep before train-time. So we sat around the miserable office and smoked pipes and tried to drink the appalling stuff that the brazen-faced hotel-keeper endeavored to palm off upon us, to deaden our moral senses and to benumb our faculties. In this condition the meanness of our nature turned upon the unhappy Passenger and Ticket Agent.

"I think," mused the lawyer, "that the next time I go fishing I shall employ a railroad man to go along, to show me all the holes and rare places."

"I have always noticed," said the doctor, "that railroad men are thoroughly informed not only as to the best fishing-grounds, but as to the season when the fish bite most freely."

"Did you ever observe," asked the lawyer, "that a railroad man never takes a private fishing-party on his own road?"

"And did it ever occur to you," replied the doctor, "that when the trip is a failure he remembers that there is a splendid place on 'our road'?"

In this agreeable strain was the conversation continued until the Passenger and Ticket Agent, a man of tact and resources, contrived to divert our minds and steer the discourse into other channels.

"Let me see," he began, "it was twenty-five — thirty — thirty-one years ago that I first came down into this country, and just thirty years ago that I left it in a hurry. I was a mere boy then, and I was trying to find rebels. Quite a party of us at the time. I remember that General Lyon was along, and that we found rebels in considerable quantities. We went back without Lyon, poor fellow, but it was mighty lively for awhile."

This started the conversation into a discussion of the battle of Wilson's Creek and the campaign in Southwest Missouri. Thence it was easy to drift into opinions concerning war in general and the present troubles. As was natural enough, those of us who had never heard a cannon, save in the way of a celebration, and couldn't tell the ping of a minie ball from the splutter of a sky-rocket, were disposed to look on war as a cheap and easy way of settling all political differences. The lawyer contended that the United States had been too lenient with Chile, and the doctor was convinced that nothing less than a thrashing would ever bring England to a proper appreciation of the Behring Sea troubles.

"Well, I don't know about that," said the Passenger and Ticket Agent, gravely; "war may be important to settle some questions, but it's my opinion that a man who has been through one war never cares to see another."

"And you're right, sir, in that opinion. War, in most cases, is a curse to humanity. In all cases it brings sorrow and suffering."

Far over in a corner of the room we had seen, when we entered, a man pushed back in a chair, with a large, soft black hat pulled over his eyes, apparently asleep. As he spoke he tilted forward, and took off his hat. He seemed to be sixty years of age, with iron gray hair and beard, and a face of strength and intelligence. A soft, somewhat smothered enunciation and the unmistakable cut of black clothes revealed the Southerner. We were a little embarrassed, for we remembered that we had spoken freely of "rebels." But we invited the stranger to come forward and have a drink, and he did so, taking one of such ample proportions as to convince us that his motives were friendly.

"You were speaking of war," he said, "though I reckon you are most of you too young to know by experience the meaning of the word. So, if you'll allow me to order up another round, I'll tell you a story."

"It's the Ancient Mariner," whispered the lawyer.

"In which event there's no use in kicking," replied the doctor.

The liquor having arrived, the stranger tossed off another alarming potion with barely a movement of the throat, a feat that lighted up the doctor's face with admiration, while a covetous look stole into his eyes as he thought of the great revelations of an autopsy. Then the stranger said, with a tone that was charming in its courtliness:

"Permit me to introduce myself. I am Major Fannin, of Texas. Perhaps the title isn't important, but down my way everybody calls me Major, and this is to be a war story."

We assured the Major, with great gravity, that in Missouri it was a luxury to address anybody under the rank of colonel, and we begged him to proceed.

"I said, when I so unceremoniously and rudely broke in upon you"—— We protested with much waving of hands. "I said that war brings sorrow and suffering. I know, for I have had both."

Strangely enough, we had not noticed until that moment that the Major's left sleeve was empty. Some men have the remarkable faculty of blinding you to their deficiencies, and the Major possessed that gift to an eminent degree.

"I am not going to offend you, gentlemen, by any opinions concerning the civil war. I was a rebel, as you call it, and one of the last to surrender. But I accepted the verdict, and am as firmly attached to-day to our common country as any of you. We'll drink together, and I'll tell you what war did for me, but we'll let the dead issues go."

Then, after a pause: "When the war broke out I was practicing law in a Texas town, married, and the father of three children, the oldest a boy of seven, the youngest a baby. The war fever seized me as it took every man and woman in the South. I'm not going to say that I ever sat down seriously to discuss principles or issues. It was enough for me that my State had decided; that my people were all of one mind and opinion. It was a fever of the most malignant type, and consequences were never thought of. In fact, I looked upon the war more as a dress parade, and when I hurried off to join my regiment I left my wife and family as gayly as if I were starting on a business trip. That was my first error and the cause of my first grief. How could I foresee the storm that raged for four years, swept away my kindred, drenched my country with blood and brought misery to my home?

"Our friend, here, spoke of coming down this way to find rebels. I reckon I was one of the rebels he found, for I remember Wilson's Creek very well, and I remember chasing bluecoats for some time after the encounter."

The laugh was on the Passenger and Ticket Agent, which he acknowledged by ordering more drinks. And the Major went on:

"It isn't necessary to the story to go into the details of my service. After the Missouri campaign I went into Kentucky and fought at Mill Spring. At Shiloh I saw my first great battle, and there I was taken prisoner. Then I began to appreciate, for the first time, the magnitude of the work we had undertaken and the extent of the Federal resources. When I was exchanged I joined Jackson's command, fought with him at Antietam and was in the great charge at Chancellorsville, where he met his death. A wonderful man that, gentlemen, a soldier and God's nobleman, every inch of him. All this time I had received vague and unsatisfactory news from home. My wife was as brave a woman as ever sent her husband to battle, but I could read between the lines a fainting spirit and a cry of despair. For the first time in my life I believe I was a coward. The night before the battle of Gettysburg I dreamed that my family were starving, and the shock of the dream unmanned me. Perhaps it turned my luck, for the next day I received my first wound; I lost this arm. Then came weeks in the hospital, and when I was able to get about again they told me, what a thousand arms could not replace, my little Jessie was dead. Jessie was my second, my favorite child. I left her a healthy little blue-eyed tot, just four years old. And the day I went to the army she came up and put her little arms around my neck, and lisped 'good-by' in her baby fashion. I kissed her as if I were going down to my office, and turned my back on her, never to see her again. They told me that she died of a slow fever, but I knew better than that, for my dream at Gettysburg came back to me. Oh, it was hard, gentlemen, it was hard!"

The old Major's voice broke and his lips were quivering. The doctor was staring uncomfortably at the ceiling, and the lawyer played nervously with the glass before him. But the railroad man, with that sort of comradeship that old soldiers have, that makes the man beholding love his fellow-man the more, put his hand on the Major's shoulder as if to steady and comfort him. The Major recovered himself and went on.

"Well, the news from home, instead of breaking me down, as they feared, put the devil in me. By this time we had begun to realize that we were fighting against terrible odds, and that the Confederacy was in a desperate way. Under ordinary circumstances I would have been dismissed as incapacitated, but the decimation of the army had been so terrible that a man with a right arm and two good legs was still worth preserving. All through the battles of the Wilderness I hung on, but Grant was pressing us, our forces were dwindling and our supplies were giving out. Day after day the cause grew more hopeless, and we saw the end coming. It came at Appomattox. That is a great and glorious word to you, gentlemen, but to me it brings up only a picture of raggedness and semi-starvation and misery.

"The conqueror told us to go home, and it seemed to me that there was a touch of irony in the word. Through the South I journeyed, the beautiful South that I had loved and fought for. How pitiable it looked, blackened by war, devastated by soldiery, the fields neglected, the homes going to ruin, the people as poor, as ragged and as miserable as myself. This, then, was the fruition of our work, the glory of the soldier's trade! As I went along my heart grew heavier. Kind words and sympathy I encountered, indeed, and such material assistance as the people could afford. And so I traveled until I reached my town, still wearing my old gray uniform, dirty and ragged, with long hair and beard and plenty of gray in both.

"I stopped before my gate, and strangers met me. They told me that Mrs. Fannin had moved to a little house in the outskirts. Just then a boy came by; it was my son, for I saw his mother in his face. He was going home, and we walked on together. Without telling him who I was, I drew from him the story of the family trials, how miserably poor they had been, how the little sister had died begging that she might see her father, and wondering why he had never come back from the office; how the servants had all run away except old Enos and Mandy, and how they had worked 'to keep the missus as 'spectable like as Mass' Henry would want.' So the boy talked and I listened with my heart in my throat until we came to the house, and I sent him in to tell his mother that a poor soldier would like to get a lodging and food.

"When my wife came to the door and I saw the care and sorrow in her face, my knees trembled so I could scarcely stand. She didn't recognize me, of course; why should she? So I spoke out and told her that I was a discharged Confederate soldier without friends, home or money, and I asked for food.

"'My poor man,' she said, 'I would give it to you gladly, but I have hardly enough for my children. My husband, like you, went to the war. God knows where he is to-day.'

"'But, madam, at least you can give me a lodging.'

"Her eyes were filled with tears. 'If I could,' she answered, 'I would do it willingly, but where can I put you away? The house is small and cramped, and I have no extra bed. I am a soldier's wife, and am almost reduced to a soldier's necessities.'

"While she was speaking a little dog that had been my dead child's favorite came around the corner of the house. He sniffed at me suspiciously and then began to caper and jump with the liveliest manifestations of joy. My children had forgotten me, my wife did not know me, but the little dog could not be deceived. I saw my wife start and look eagerly into my face, and I cried out:

"'Mary, don't you know me?'

"And just then old Mandy came to the door and threw up both hands and exclaimed:

"'Fo' God, it's Mass' Henry come back!'

"Well, we all went into the wretched little house and sat down and cried for joy. The baby, now the image of the little Jessie I had left, came bashfully in and caught hold of my empty sleeve, at which my wife cried the more. We sat up half the night, and she told me all her griefs and troubles, though I have always suspected that she softened them as much as possible. And she brought out a little package and kissed it and put it into my hands without a word. I opened it. It was a lock of little Jessie's hair."

The Major paused and studied the floor for a moment. Then he said: "It was up-hill work, but I have been successful. My sorrow ended with that reunion. There isn't a happier home in Texas, nor one that looks with greater abhorrence upon the curse of war."

The lawyer whispered to the landlord. As he came back with the glasses, the lawyer said:

"Major, you've converted me. I'll give you a toast. Peace, enduring peace!"

The old Major stood up, and very handsome and soldierly he looked. He bowed to us as he said:

"And the Union!"

The railroad man, who had fought at Wilson's Creek, reached over and clasped his hand.

Sweetheart.

SWEETHEART.

FARMER ROOKS sat on the fence, smoking his pipe and looking complacently over his acres, which stretched away a mile to the south of the important town of Primrose.

Every student of border history must be familiar with the chronicles of Primrose, its early scenes of frontier deviltry, its famous rebellion against Kansas State authority and its bloody county-seat war with Hellbent, which cost thousands of dollars and scores of lives, and was the moving cause of one of the most prosperous graveyards between Topeka and the Rockies. Farmer Rooks was not a farmer in those stirring times. In fact, it would be difficult to say precisely what his occupation was. He had drifted into Kansas apparently for the humor of the thing, and for a year or two devoted himself to the liquor interest in the way of consumption, and to such ephemeral pleasure as can be gathered from association with cowboys in their hours of relaxation. When the county was organized and the question of a county seat came up, young Rooks took the stump for Primrose, his natural abilities and education giving him the qualifications for leadership. It was he who first pointed out the absurdity and disgrace that would attend the selection of a town with the name of Hellbent. To counteract the effect of this speech the people of Hellbent immediately called a public meeting and changed the name to Benthell. But the reform was not adequate, and a majority of voters decided in favor of Primrose. Then the bad men of Hellbent organized a raid, and one dark and otherwise advantageous night swooped down on Primrose and captured the records. Rooks immediately called in his friends, the cowboys, and returned the raid and the compliment. And so the feud ran on for a year, until Hellbent was practically depopulated and Rooks was a curiosity of perforations. At last an honorable treaty of peace was agreed upon, and Primrose was permitted to retain the spoils of conquest.

In return for his efficient services Rooks was invited to claim any amount of honors and emoluments. But a man who has been probed in every part of his body naturally loses a taste for active life and harassing duties. So he compromised on a testimonial banquet at the "Delmonico restaurant," and went into the business of agriculture on the outskirts of the town. His first graceful act was to go over to Hellbent and espouse the belle of the defeated tribe, thereby completely healing the breach and setting an honorable example to future Montagues and Capulets. As Primrose prospered, so also did Farmer Rooks and his charming and thrifty bride, barring the one deplorable grasshopper invasion and an occasional hot wind that the ingenuity of man is not able to circumvent.

In spite of her arduous duties and the many pressing demands upon her time and attention, the erstwhile belle of Hellbent found occasion to present to her husband the most charming and delightful miniature edition of herself. This incident, though it was by no means unparalleled in Primrose, which was beginning to experience a steady and reliable increase in population, created much local enthusiasm. The entire town journeyed to the Rooks farm, and the men shook hands with the happy father, while the ladies made minute observations and the most critical examination, and all agreed that such a baby was a special dispensation of Providence and an unprecedented manifestation of favor to Primrose. A corner lot was immediately voted by the town authorities, and called, by way of pleasantry and gentle reminder, Rooks's First Addition.

Now, when it came to the point of naming this important young personage, Farmer Rooks and his wife had their first falling-out. The mother was not too particular, and selected from her family stock a large variety of names which Farmer Rooks rejected as being altogether commonplace and unworthy. Like a loyal son, he would have remembered his own mother, but Hannah — that was too much. They lay awake nights quarreling over the vexatious point. They sent into town for a dictionary, and went carefully and laboriously over the Scripture proper names and the Greek and Latin proper names and the Christian names of women and the noted names of fiction, and even the modern geographical names, but with no result. The schoolmaster and the minister came to their assistance, and the minister prayed very fervently that God would aid them in making a decision; but, despite the assurance of assistance, the name was as far away as ever. At one time Farmer Rooks was favorably inclined to Leda, but the schoolmaster, who was a very young man, blushed a great deal and hastily convinced the father that he was contemplating a great wrong to an innocent child. Farmer Rooks admitted that he knew nothing of mythology, and warmly thanked the young schoolmaster for extricating him from a grave peril.

All this time the baby was growing and developing at a famous rate, and seemed to look with reproachful wonder out of its big blue eyes at the unhappy parents, who bade fair to send her nameless through life. When Farmer Rooks went to the field, he took the little dictionary with him, and over and over again the wondering horses heard his "Abigail, Adeline, Adelaide, Agatha — git up, there!— Clara, Clarissa, Constance, Cora — w-h-o-a!— Arethusa, Asteria, Athena, Aurora — g'long, now — Ceres, Diana — back! who-a!" And at night the mother, washing the dishes, would take up the sad refrain: "Octavia, Olivia, Pauline, Penelope — Hiram, did you fetch in the wood?— Sophia, Sophronia, Stella, Susanna — there's the baby, Hiram!"

One day Farmer Rooks sat in the kitchen on the wood-box. It was raining hard, the baby had no name, and the world was very black. There came a sound as of a falling weight, and a loud squall proclaimed that the baby had tumbled out of her crib. Then the mother's voice was heard: "What's the matter, sweetheart? Who's been hurting mamma's little sweetheart?"

Farmer Rooks jumped from the wood-box and slapped his leg. "By gad, Nell, found at last! You've struck it this time. We'll call her Sweetheart!"

Great news always travels quickly, and twenty-four hours had not elapsed before the whole town knew that the baby had been named. At first some carping complaints were heard. The minister's wife argued that such a name would not tend to the spiritual advancement of the child; that she would grow up in vanity and self-consciousness, and that her mind would be filled with distracting thoughts before her time. A few other mothers resented the monopoly implied by the name, and hinted that there was likely to be a good deal more than one "sweetheart" in the community. But Farmer Rooks was obstinate. He maintained forcefully that it was his child and he could call her whatever he chose. She was "Sweetheart" to him and would always be. If other people did not like the name they could call her Miss Rooks. This appeared to strike the community as a perfectly reasonable suggestion, and an exhibition of Rooks's usual good, hard sense.

As Sweetheart grew up all opposition to the name, as to its propriety or appropriateness, melted away. It was a sure case of love at first sight, and everybody who saw her surrendered on the spot. The Rooks farm was on the main road to Benthell and High Rock, and nobody in the county thought of driving by without pulling up to catch a glimpse of Sweetheart. She was the only child, for Mrs. Rooks, who was a busy woman, had discovered that the demands and cares of maternity were entirely too exacting for a farmer's wife in an undeveloped country. Consequently, she was all the more precious to the farmer's heart, and he never wearied of repeating her epigrams when he went to town, and of exhibiting her accomplishments to the stranger within the gates.

Mrs. Rooks, on the other hand, did not share in this manner of adoration. She admitted her daughter's beauty and many good qualities, but was not blind to the little eccentricities which are part of a child's nature. Mrs. Rooks had, moreover, forcible theories of government, and had established a set of by-laws which are found in every well-regulated household. Consequently, Sweetheart's life was not wholly devoid of those exciting and purely one-sided or jug-handled episodes which befall all children of high animal spirits. These interviews Mrs. Rooks described as "molding the character," but it was significant that Sweetheart's character was never "molded" when her father was at home, for he countenanced no liberties with Sweetheart's feelings.

So the years went peacefully by until the early afternoon when, as hereinbefore related, Farmer Rooks sat on the fence and smoked his pipe and looked over his acres. It was the end of an old-fashioned winter, and spring had come on with one of those lightning changes that are the perplexities of agricultural life in Kansas. Farmer Rooks was too old a settler to be misled by any climatic blandishments, and the mercury that stood at 75 on an April afternoon, with a hot wind blowing from the southwest, offered no inducements for rash experiments. Near the farmer little Sweetheart was disporting with all the enthusiasm of her five years and exercising the petty tyrannies that a child has in store for a completely subjugated father. Farmer Rooks looked at her admiringly, and chuckled at the reflection that he had the prettiest child, the thriftiest wife, the tidiest home and the best farm in the county. "Such a figure as that child has," he laughed to himself: "as plump as a prairie chicken and as graceful as a colt." In truth, Sweetheart was a pretty picture as she romped up and down the yard, her cheeks rosy with the color of health, her blue eyes dancing with childish glee, and her flaxen curls blown all over her head by the force of the wind. But it might have been noticed that in her play she was particularly careful to see that no accident befell the new shoes on her little feet, for just before the outing Mrs. Rooks had requested an interview with Sweetheart, and had told her that if anything happened to those shoes something would drop. What that something was the child had distinct and painful recollection.

"I'm going into town, mother," said the farmer, calling to the busy woman in the kitchen. "You keep an eye on Sweetheart, as she's like to blow away. If the wind doesn't let up before night we may hear from it."

So Farmer Rooks jumped on his horse and cantered off to town, with numerous commissions from the infant tyrant, which he gravely jotted down on the back of an old envelope. Sweetheart watched him to the end of the potato-patch and returned to her sports. She was doubtless playing one of those mysterious and intricate games that are evolved from a child's process of thought, which consist of a great deal of digging in the dirt and accumulation of small lumber and other accessories. All the afternoon she devoted to this occult scheme of diversion, contemplating a great surprise for the farmer, and pausing anon to inspect the condition of the new shoes.

Neither the busy woman in the house nor the child at play noticed the change in the atmosphere. The wind had died away and the air was hot and oppressive. At times the sky seemed to give a yellow light; then almost as quickly it would take a greenish tinge, which would as rapidly fade away. There was no signal service expert in Primrose, and there were no weather prophets to guess at probabilities, but the big rooster that strutted up and down past the little girl cocked his eye occasionally at the heavens as much as to say: "I don't like the looks of things, Sweetheart; you and I'd better get out of this."

Sweetheart had reached that point in her architectural pursuits when it became necessary to get up and stand off at a little distance and scrutinize her work. At that moment there came from the distance a low, dull roar, and the big rooster gave a quick squawk of alarm and ran to the shed. The mother in the kitchen heard it, and came to the door, but there stood Sweetheart with her eyes upon her castle and her thoughts wrapped up in the surprise for her father. Straight from the southwest, skirting the edge of the town, and coming at an incredible speed, was a huge balloon, and Sweetheart, looking up, saw it and clapped her hands with joy. One look, however, made the mother's heart stand still. She knew too well now the meaning of the distant roaring and the fate of whatever stood in the path of the monster that bounded up and down and swept on in its course of death. "Sweetheart!" she screamed, and took one step forward. She was too late. The cloud was on them with an angry shriek, and in a second everything was swept away. The house was in ruins; the sheds were flattened like cardboard; great trees were torn up and twisted, and the air was filled with flying timbers and household articles. Pinned to the earth, the mother lay as one dead. And Sweetheart — where was Sweetheart?

Farmer Rooks sat in the grocery on a nail-box with a dozen of his friends about him. "You see," said he, "mother and I took Sweetheart over to the Higginses to call on Joe's folks. And while we were there Joe's wife's baby got hungry and she had to nurse it. Sweetheart all the time looking on

with her eyes wide open. And when we were
going home Sweetheart says: 'Mamma, I don't
think that was a nice thing for Mrs. Higgins to do.
I think it was nasty.' And her mother said:
'Why, Sweetheart, you and I used to do that when
you were a little baby.' And Sweetheart put on a
look of great disgust, and said: 'Well, mamma, if
I did, for heaven's sake don't say anything about
it!'"

A great shout greeted this story, and just then
Bill Harper, the butcher, rushed in and cried out:
"Boys, there's a cyclone south o' town, and it
looks as if it might strike your place, Hi!"

Pell-mell they crowded into the street. Farmer
Rooks's face was ghastly pale, and he shook like a
leaf. Away to the northeast they saw that angry,
bounding balloon, and marked the ruin in its wake.
Another minute, and Farmer Rooks was in the saddle and off in a dead run, and those who looked on
his face saw an agony that was indescribable.

"Boys," said Bill Harper, "it's got Rooks's place,
sure; it was right in the line of the cyclone. God
help him if we can't; but we'll try."

Men on horseback and men in wagons followed
Farmer Rooks, who was now far ahead and riding
like a demon. Within a quarter of a mile of his
farm he saw the house was gone. He reeled and
nearly fell from the saddle. But the horse seemed
to realize the pressure of his mission, and ran

madly on through the rain, now falling in a torrent, evading and clearing the limbs and branches of trees that lay across his path. In front of where was once the door the animal stopped, and Farmer Rooks threw himself from his back, and knelt by the side of his wife.

"Mother! mother!" he cried. "Where is Sweetheart?"

A few minutes later, when the neighbors and friends drove up, they found him looking among the ruins and moaning, "Oh, Sweetheart, Sweetheart!"

It was an easy task to release the farmer's wife, and the work of a minute to restore her to consciousness. Her left arm was broken, but she couldn't think of that. She saw her husband prying among the timbers, and she heard his moans of anguish, and knew that Sweetheart was gone. She could tell nothing. The storm had come like a flash and swept her away from her side.

"One thing is sure," said Billy Sedgwick, "the child isn't here, and has been carried off by the wind. We'll have to foller the path till we find her."

They went out very solemnly, for they knew they were going after the dead. And those who had little girls at home turned away their heads so that Hi mightn't see the tears in their eyes. But

Farmer Rooks was hurrying along with that deadly pallor still on his face, and his wife, forgetful of her broken arm, was at his side. Her lips were moving, and Bill Harper said she was praying.

Then Bill Sedgwick and Jim Grant and the Kingman boys, who were in front, set up a shout. And here came Sweetheart up the road. Her little dress was in tatters, her stockings were down, and one shoe was gone. Her flaxen curls were torn and dirty, her face was streaked with mud, and, withal, she was well plastered from head to foot. The mother, in a manner perfectly characteristic of her sex, no sooner saw her child alive than she gave a shriek and fainted away. The father rushed to the little one and grabbed her up and kissed her muddy hair and dirty face and little scratched arms again and again.

"I didn't run away, papa," said Sweetheart, apologetically. "I didn't want to go. But when the big balloon came along somebody reached down and grabbed me up and held me tight so I couldn't get away, and he took me off down the road with a lot of boards and things and our speckled hen and the red chicken-coop. And after awhile he got tired and laughed and let me down in a mud-puddle and splashed me all over; and — and " (here she looked fearfully at her mother, who was coming to consciousness) "I — I — losted one of my shoes."

But the father took little Sweetheart in his arms and pressed her to his breast. And, forgetful of his ruined home and blighted farm, he buried his face in her tangled curls and sobbed for joy and thankfulness. For now he knew that God had ridden on the storm.

The Political Wanderings of Joseph Macon.

THE POLITICAL WANDERINGS OF JOSEPH MACON.

The door of the little back room was carefully closed, and the Numidian attendant was instructed to see that the company was not disturbed.

"There is great danger in making a Kentucky toddy," said Colonel Bollinger, as the boys drew around the table and surveyed the preparations with interest. "You take a lump of sugar, like this, put it in a long glass, and pour in a very little water, just enough to dissolve the sugar. Then you stir with a spoon, and add the whisky. Complete by pouring in more water."

"But where's the danger, Colonel?"

"The danger, sir, is in getting in too much water. You may not believe it, but to make a toddy as it should be made is one of the most puzzling of all the glorious arts of modern times. I remember when Joe Macon came down to visit me that we sat up together half the night experimenting. Joe would never admit that we had discovered the secret of exact proportion, and the result was that when we started for home, although we had only three blocks to go, we must have covered half a mile of territory. And when a policeman I happened to know offered to assist Joe, he told him that he didn't require assistance, as everybody knew that the longest way round was the shortest way home."

"Who was Joe Macon, Colonel?"

"Joe Macon, sir, was one of the greatest politicians this country has ever known, as cunning as a fox, as strong as an ox, and as brave as a lion. If one of you gentlemen will ring for the cigars I'll tell you a story about him. Thanks—a Henry Clay, please, rather strong.

"Well, when the war broke out, Joe was living up in Northwest Missouri, a sort of dealer in general merchandise, sugar, coffee, clothing, niggers, and the like. Andy Callaway and Joe married sisters, daughters of old Squire Benton, who was with Price during the troubles in this State. Andy was a right smart sort of fellow himself, and what he didn't know about a nigger trade couldn't be learned. Of course his sympathies were all with the South, and at first he promised the squire that he'd join the army. But the more he got to thinking about it the less he liked the idea. You see, all of Andy's property was up among the Dutch, and if he joined the rebel army it meant confiscation and a dead loss. So Andy closed out his niggers and went home to think it over."

The Colonel bit off the end of his cigar and

chuckled. "Well, the first thing Joe knew, along came the Home Guards one day, and here marched Andy with a lot of Dutchmen, dressed up in a blue uniform and carrying the Union flag, with the band playing Yankee Doodle, or some other odious air. Joe was mad clear way through, and, when Andy looked over at him and winked, Joe wanted to go and pull him out of the ranks. But his wife said: 'You let Andy Callaway alone. Depend upon it, he knows what he's doing.' That night Andy came over to Joe's house, still wearing his blue uniform. That made Joe madder than ever, and the way he lit into Andy was a caution. But Andy just sat and grinned, and when Joe had finished he said:

"'Now look here, Joe, you're on the wrong track. It's all well enough for us to be talking about our sympathies and our rights, but the fact is it's a question whether we'll go broke or keep our property and our skins. As a choice between the Dutch and a rope or a bullet, I'll take the Dutch. And if you're sensible you'll go with me.'

"Much to Joe's surprise, his wife spoke up and warmly seconded Andy. Mrs. Macon was a thrifty woman, and as she lived in a border State she didn't have much of that impractical sentiment that was so popular among the women further South. And Andy kept pegging away at him.

"'The thing for you to do, Joe, is to go up to

the hall with me to-morrow night and make application for membership in the Home Guards.'

"'What good will that do?' said Joe. 'Everybody in the country knows that I've owned and sold niggers, and that I'm a rebel. They'll just laugh at me and perhaps mob me.'

"'No, they won't,' said Andy; 'I'll tell you exactly what they'll do. When you send in your name Jim Cole will be there. He kicks at everything and everybody. It's more than likely that he'll get up and denounce you, and when he gets to calling you names you want to go for him right off. Knock him down and lick him. That'll tickle the Dutch and be a sure proof of your loyalty, and they'll take you right in.'

"Well, they talked and argued and wrangled, and finally Joe gave in and allowed he'd try it, anyway. And the more he thought of it the better-humored he became. And he tried on Andy's coat and strutted up and down the room, and as he thought of the wrath of his father-in-law he laughed till the tears ran down his cheeks.

"So the next night Andy came around and got Joe, and they went up together to the hall. The boys looked mighty curious when they saw Joe come in, for you see Joe had talked pretty loud about nigger-loving Yankees, and it was generally known that he had fitted one fellow out and sent him off to Price. But Andy and Joe sat down and didn't say a word until it came time to nominate new members. Then Andy got up and made a little speech. He said it gave him great pleasure to propose his brother-in-law, Joseph Macon, as a member of the company. He supposed that it was pretty well known to the intelligent and representative Germans present that Mr. Macon's early sympathies, like his own, had been with the Confederacy. But since the South had so far forgotten itself as to fire on the flag, that glorious emblem of a great and honored union of States, he had felt it his duty to rally to its defense. He therefore begged the privilege of enrollment among the other honorable defenders of the Union.

"When Andy sat down there was faint applause, and, sure enough, Jim Cole, who had been sneering all through his speech, took the floor. Jim was a sarcastic fellow, and he began by saying that he highly approved such loyal sentiments coming from so authoritative a source. He was glad to hear that Mr. Macon had experienced this revulsion of feeling, for less than twenty-four hours before he had heard the gentleman cursing the Union from Abe Lincoln down to the janitor of the Rhode Island State-house. For his own part he knew Mr. Macon to be the all-firedest rebel in Northwest Missouri, an unrepentant nigger-trader and a man who would cut up a blue uniform for dish-rags.

"Well, these spirited remarks set up a great

hubbub among the Dutch, for Jim was an authority on the question of loyalty. And Andy nudged Joe as a sort of hint that the crisis had come. So Joe got up very deliberately and remarked that he was greatly pained and outraged by these aspersions on his patriotism. He apologized to the company for his inability to make a speech, and said that, as a man of action and not of words, he would detain them only a moment. Then he crossed over to Jim Cole and said: 'Jim, you're the durnedest liar in the town, and I can prove it.' With that he hit him between the eyes and knocked him flat, picked him up and threw him over three rows of chairs, stood him up again and kicked him six or eight times, and finally left him in a heap in the corner. Then he turned to the company and roared: 'If there's any other gentleman has anything to say ag'in me or the Union, now's his call.'

"Of course nobody had anything to say in the face of this argument, and Joe was taken right into membership before Jim had fairly come to consciousness. You couldn't have made a Dutchman in that room believe that Joe wasn't next thing to an abolitionist."

"Was Joe a good Union man after that, Colonel?"

"Union man?" echoed the Colonel, with great scorn. "He was one of the best Union men you ever saw. He'd go down to the meetings and listen to the proceedings, and then ride all night to warn one of his Confederate friends who had been marked for arrest. He was such a Union man that he couldn't bear to think that the Union should be put to the trouble and expense of supporting a worthless rebel."

The Colonel puffed a moment in silence. "Poor Andy," he went on, "he didn't have much show after all. One day the news came that the rebels were in the neighborhood, and the Home Guards were called out. In some way, while they were dodging back of town, the boys got scattered and divided. Two squads came up on one another in the brush and got to firing. Before they found out their mistake Andy was killed. Joe always claimed that it wasn't a mistake at all; that they killed him out of pure malice. They took him back to town and gave him a military funeral, and covered the coffin with the stars and stripes, and put *Dulce est pro patria mori* in his obituary. Joe tells me that not long ago Andy's wife received a pension with back money as a slight testimonial from a grateful country."

"What became of Joe?"

"Well, Joe settled down to farming after the war. But he didn't make much of a success of it. He was too great a man. Perhaps you've noticed that a great man is only great between spells of farming. Cincinnatus was that kind. His farming merely gave him a chance to think up more greatness. Joe was a natural politician. He would hang around and find out how things were going, and then he'd go that way. He used to say that he wouldn't trust a man who wasn't open to conviction. But somehow Joe was unlucky. When he ran as a Republican the county went Democratic, and when he came out as a Democrat the county flopped over and went Republican. If he got on the Prohibition ticket the county went wet, and he no sooner took the side of the antis than every Dutchman voted dry. It was the most curious thing you ever saw. Yet Joe was a brainy man, and one of the best wire-pullers in the State. But he did have such luck. One day he started to bring in a lot of section hands, at his own expense, on a gravel train. The engine jumped the track, and Joe and his brother didn't reach town till three hours after the polls closed. Joe was beaten by one majority. Another time he imported a lot of Irishmen from Kansas and kept them for two weeks. On election-day they all got drunk and went fishing. There never was anything like it for luck.

"Naturally, Joe got a little discouraged. His farm began to play out, as farms will when they are run as political annexes, and his wife and children were considerably annoyed by malaria. So Joe reckoned he'd pull up and quit. It looked a little inviting over on the Kansas side, and he moved across and purchased a few acres near the river. There was plenty of good land cheap a few miles back in the country, but Joe said he was tired and didn't like to travel, anyhow, and he thought he'd try it around the edge, just to see how Kansas was going to suit. If he liked it, he could dip a little farther in any time.

"Well, with Joe's record as a Union soldier, and on the strength of his fracas with Jim Cole, he could have had a good thing in Kansas. But here is where his confounded luck came in again. Just about this time Cleveland was elected President, and Joe took it into his head that he wanted to be postmaster. Of course, that killed him with the Republicans, and the fight over the office grew so hot that the party was disrupted, and two-thirds of the Democratic leaders had it in for Joe. To crown his sorrows, another fellow got the office, and the next year the river rose and washed out his farm. Then Joe gave up, and took to drink, which he had sort of been taking to pretty naturally for some years. His wife died, and his daughters married off, and it left him free to do about as he pleased. He was such a good-natured fellow that everybody liked him, and he was always sergeant-at-arms at Democratic conventions on account of his great strength and his love of order.

"Down in Joe's neighborhood the county invariably had its final Democratic rally of the campaign. The boys would gather from all quarters, build a huge camp-fire and circle around it while the speaking was going on. Every man was supposed to bring his own private jug of Jeffersonian doctrine, and as the meeting never adjourned until the doctrine gave out there was a good deal of oratory. At such times Joe was in his element, and always saw that everything was pleasant and harmonious.

"That reminds me," said the Colonel, "that I am getting a little parched. Beg pardon. You were about to order the drinks when I interrupted you. No, my boy, not for the world; you spoke first. I shall be happy to drink with you."

When he had measurably refreshed himself, the Colonel proceeded:

"I remember being present at one of these rallies. I was invited to address the County Democracy on the character of Jefferson. Although I was a stranger to most of the statesmen assembled, they honored me with profound attention, and, I may say with modesty, unstinted applause. When we first met together around the fire, I noticed with displeasure that there was a nigger present, not as a servant, which would have been perfectly proper, but as a Democrat and a brother. I spoke to two or three gentlemen about it, but as they seemed to treat it with indifference, I could not, as a guest, object. For a time the greatest harmony prevailed, but as the toasts grew more frequent and the good liquor began to circulate, I could observe a marked change in the demeanor of the crowd. Occasionally a gentleman would look up and catch sight of the nigger, and a look of astonishment would come over his face, as if he observed him for the first time. And by and by the whole crowd began to scrutinize the nigger in an aggrieved and injured way, not exactly in a hostile manner, but with that air which suggests perplexity, annoyance, inability to account for the presence of an interloper.

"As I recall it, Judge Gentry, as grand a Democrat as ever drew the breath of life, was speaking of the comprehensive principles of Democracy. The fire had burned low, and we were unable to distinguish faces around the circle. The Judge had reached an eloquent climax in which he glorified the equality of man as sustained by the Democracy, and thanked God that we had met that night as brothers in a grand universal brotherhood, when there came the sound of two quick blows, and a man tumbled back into the fire. As he fell, the embers, displaced by the body, shot up a sudden flame, and we recognized the features of the nigger. And, do you know, as a most remarkable example of spontaneity of thought, every man in that circle jumped to his feet and shouted:

'Hurrah for Joe Macon!' It was one of the grandest, most inspiring sights I ever witnessed. Judge Gentry told me that, in all his forty years of labor for the Democratic party, he had never observed a more thrilling tribute to a party worker."

"Did they send him to Congress, Colonel?"

"No, sir; poor Joe was too far gone at that time to receive any reward, however merited. A few months later he was taken into the Soldiers' Home, that beautiful haven of rest prepared by our country for those who have fought her battles. I spent a Sunday with him. As I came up the walk from the station, here was Joe jabbering with a couple of old fellows in blue, and drawing in the gravel with his cane. He was saying: 'Now, it was just like this at Bull's Run. Here were the rebels over here in the woods, and here was our command down by the stream that ran along this way.'

"When I had him alone I said: 'Joe, what were you talking about, you old rascal? You know that you never were at Bull's Run.'

"And Joe looked at me in a doubtful sort of way, and said: 'Colonel, I've told that —— lie so many times since I've been here that I'm gettin' to believe it myself.'"

The Distribution.

THE DISTRIBUTION.

It is related in the brief chronicles of the adventures of Moses in Egypt that, after the law-giver, with Divine assistance, had subjected Pharaoh to various annoyances such as murrain of beasts, tremendous crops of frogs and flies, painful boils and blains and a visitation of hail, he caused a shower of locusts that not only covered the land and ate up every green thing, but superinduced the bold statement that "before them there were no such locusts as they, neither after them shall be such." Doubtless, Moses was perfectly honest in this opinion, for, prophet as he was, he could not foresee the possibilities of the great American continent. Indeed, all Christian lands have accepted this promise with a security that argued well for their faith; but, in an evil moment for Moses, people began to move into Kansas. Now Kansas has always prided itself on its ability as a record-breaker, and, despite the orthodox religious sentiment there prevalent, it is doubtful whether it has ever regarded Moses as a leader in the same class with John Brown. And as for Pharaoh's little experience with the locusts, you can get thousands of affidavits in Kansas any day to the effect that a Mosaic locust is to a Kansas grasshopper what a humming-bird is to a sparrow-hawk. These affidavits are not intended to be irreverent or unorthodox, but are merely the outgrowth of patriotism and State pride.

In fact, the Kansas man, having rallied from the plague, is as proud of his grasshopper as a woman is of her pet poodle. The Egyptian article subsisted on green things, but the Kansas variety is claimed to have devoured cord-wood, kitchen utensils and bits of scrap-iron and nails; in truth, everything except the mortgage, which thus far seems to have escaped even the ingenuity of Providence. Whoever visits Kansas in these days should not fail to ask the inhabitant to tell him about the iron pot half-devoured by the ravenous insects, or the crowbar into which they burrowed in their efforts to make a square meal. These things are now among the sacred traditions of the State, and will be properly attested before a notary. When one sits down to write of them, he cannot avoid the conviction that Pharaoh's trouble has been very greatly overestimated.

Nobody contends that the Lord sent the grasshopper into Kansas, as previously He showered the locusts upon Egypt. If any significance of divine motive appears in this visitation, it is that He afflicted Kansas as, many centuries before, He visited sorrow upon Job — a test of strength and forbearance. At least this is the popular Kansas idea, and it is entitled to consideration.

After all, there is much that is compensatory in the workings of Providence, and while the Lord sent the grasshoppers as a sort of gentle reminder that the Kansas man was putting on more airs than the average farmer is entitled to under a high protective tariff, he had compromised the blow by granting a wheat crop of sufficient yield to prevent a disastrous season of infidelity. And then, as this concession appeared to be too strong an evidence of favor and discrimination against Job, he gave the devil permission to supplement the grasshopper pest with a drought that ate up the farmer's patience as neatly as the insects devoured his grain. Such was the condition of affairs at Dobbins the morning after the grasshopper convention and banquet.

Dobbins had never figured very extensively in the political history of Kansas, partly because it was a new town and partly because its settlers had not had the advantage of previous training in Ohio or Indiana. It had never turned out anything more formidable in a political way than a candidate for the Legislature, and he had been beaten by a combination which Judge Jefferson always referred to as "circumstances."

Judge Thomas Jefferson, or the "Jedge," as he

was familiarly called, was the one character in Dobbins who, everybody conceded, had been strangely and harshly neglected by fate. To the simple people among whom he lived he was a mine of information and learning, a vast repository of facts and figures. To him went all the neighbors with questions and problems, and it is due to the Judge to say that he answered them promptly with great facility. It was largely through the Judge's aptness in answering questions off-hand that for a time the idea prevailed in certain circles of Dobbins that Leviticus was a Roman general. And when the minister sought to dispel this illusion the Judge explained, with great impressiveness, that there were two distinct branches of the family, the Hebrew and the Roman, and that he had naturally supposed that the question referred to the modern representative who had distinguished himself by his great gallantry in the second Punic war. "Oh, well," said the Judge, in the off-hand way that characterizes men of great erudition, "if you mean the Hebrew fellow, I suppose the parson's right." And as the Judge pronounced the word with the accent on the first syllable the impression grew that Leviticus was an old Mosaic humorist. So the Judge emerged from the argument with greater prestige than before.

The Judge had moved into Kansas from Missouri at the close of the civil war, and had settled down on Dry Creek, which subsequently marked the southern limits of the town of Dobbins. It was confidently believed by his fellow-citizens that in Missouri he had been a distinguished jurist, and that he had been obliged to fly from home on account of his loyalty to the Union and for the reason that old Caspar's father left Blenheim—they burnt his dwelling to the ground. This impression the Judge never undertook to correct. But in Kansas he was content to live on his past reputation, and to make ends meet with such little manual labor as a small gentleman farmer could with dignity allow.

The early history of Judge Jefferson was a sealed book. Indeed, the gentleman himself avoided all inquiries tending to lead up to personal matters, and at such times bore so unmistakable a look of pain that it was admitted by common consent that he was the hero of a mystery; but whether a romance or a lynching, it was impossible to tell. When he had first appeared on Dry Creek, he had been distinguished for his long, luxuriant hair and an expansive shirt front. In later years he had curtailed his locks, but retained the prestige of exposing a wider area of shirt bosom than any man in the district. In politics he was, as his name would indicate, a Democrat, and while this fact did not deprive him of any social pleasures, it proved a barrier to the realization of those hopes that at one time or another inflame every voter in Kansas. "In this world," said the Judge, "I am a martyr to principle, but in the great and notable day of the Lord I shall find my recompense."

As Dobbins grew the Judge began to branch out. He it was who opened the first real estate office, organized the first town-lot company, and called the attention of Eastern capitalists to the golden opportunities that were waiting to be picked up along Dry Creek. It was the Judge who presided at all the public meetings, made the most stirring public-spirited addresses, and cheerfully gave his time and his eloquence to offset the cash contributions of those less gifted and less influential.

Yet in spite of these exertions and this laudable display of public spirit Dobbins remained a village, and the Judge showed no evidence of prosperity. In fact, the little farm on the creek began to run down, and the Judge's shirt bosom, never of immaculate whiteness, bore tobacco stains somewhat deeper and more numerous than before. Things looked squally for the descendant of the great patriot.

One day a letter came saying that the Judge's wife had come into possession of a three-hundred-dollar legacy through the timely demise of a superfluous relative. In honor of this felicitous event, the next day being the Sabbath of the Lord, the

Judge gave a dinner-party to his daughters and sons-in-law, his sons and daughters-in-law, and their heirs and assigns of all ages. The older members of the family were still sitting at the table, and the heirs and assigns were playing in the yard, when there came a tap, tap, tap at the window pane. The Judge had reached a point in his discourse where he was disposing of the last hundred dollars of the legacy, and he looked annoyed by the interruption.

"It's only the children," said his wife, soothingly.

"As I was saying," went on the Judge, "I mean to take this last portion of the money and apply it to "—— And again came the tap, tap, tap. The Judge looked over his spectacles to catch the culprits at the window, but they were not in sight. "To take this money and apply it to the improvement of the "—— And for the third time, and louder than before, came the tap, tap, tap.

"Bill," said the Judge, "I wish you'd go out and drive those children away. This money came to us lawfully, and it seems as though we might have the privilege of disposing of it as we please."

Bill rose carelessly and went to the door. He opened it and looked out. Then he closed it quickly and turned to the old man with his face white.

"My God, father, it's grasshoppers!"

The company jumped from the table and rushed to the door and windows. A cloud of insects almost shut out the sky, and thousands had already settled down on the trees and ripening grain. Even as the startled farmers looked the vegetation seemed to disappear, and, as if in a moment, the valley was like a prairie swept by fire or a country sacked and pillaged by the conquerors in war. The Judge looked first at the destroyers and then at his sons. "Boys," said he, "we're busted, by ——!"

A less indomitable spirit than Thomas Jefferson, the namesake and descendant of the man who constructed the cradle of liberty, would have been crushed by this misfortune. But the Judge was unconquerable. In fact, he experienced a glow of pleasure, as it were, in the reflection that at last he was a "sufferer." The old-time Kansan exults in "suffering." He esteems it a natural stage through which he must pass in order to reach the true dignity of life. A life in Kansas without some of the cruel tests and disappointments that beset a new country is to subject the citizen to suspicion and distrust, and to cause him to be looked upon as a Sybarite and an enemy to existing conditions. So the Judge, with a flutter of pride, mounted his horse, which the grasshoppers had spared, and rode to town.

The ruin had been so widespread that the Judge soon found himself in the company of the most prosperous farmers of the valley, and it required very little argument to convince them that the calamity was one that appealed directly to the sympathy and charity of the entire nation.

"As one who has been prostrated by this heavy blow," said the Judge, "I shall take the liberty of calling a public meeting, to be held in the Methodist church to-morrow afternoon, to devise means to lay our misfortunes properly before the country."

When the Judge called this meeting to order the church was filled with sufferers and their friends. The Judge began with great dignity. He reminded his hearers that their misfortune was not unparalleled; that the Romans, returning from the second Punic war, had found their crops devastated by a similar pest. Should the citizens of Dobbins be less courageous than the people of Rome? Should they not bear up under their affliction, at the same time setting forth the exact facts in order that the country might not be debarred from the blessed privilege of giving of its store?

Jim Hodgman demurred. Jim had always looked upon the Judge as a Missouri mossback, and thwarted him in every possible way. He admitted that he didn't know anything about a Punic war, or what the Romans did, but when he was in Kansas he believed in doing as the Kansans did. He had looked around the room, and while there were some honest farmers present, the meeting was composed largely of men who couldn't be hurt by a dozen grasshopper invasions. For his own part, he had raised a good crop of wheat, and was in no danger of starving. He moved the meeting adjourn.

The Judge replied with great eloquence and fervor. He submitted to the council of "sturdy farmers and their friends" that a cry of distress was going up all over Kansas; that the great newspapers of the country would be filled with dispatches from every county and town. Could Dobbins afford to miss this glorious opportunity to advertise itself in the Eastern press?

Mr. Hodgman asked, with a slight shade of sarcasm, if that was the policy adopted by the suffering Romans after the second Punic war.

Judge Jefferson answered with spirit that the facilities of the old Romans were somewhat abridged, but that they were great hands to take advantage of their opportunities.

Tom Meade thought that Dobbins would acquire a better measure of advertising by taking care of itself and declining all offers of assistance. This opinion created a flutter and great agitation on the part of the Jefferson contingent.

Mr. Hodgman renewed his motion to adjourn.

The motion was lost, and a committee was appointed to draft resolutions setting forth the calamity that had overtaken the Dry Creek Valley and the town of Dobbins, and imploring such assistance as a generous nation could grant. At his own suggestion Judge Jefferson was selected to go to Kansas City to stir up the Board of Trade to a realization of the disaster. Thereupon the meeting adjourned, subject to the call of the chairman of the executive committee.

That great director of public sentiment, the Dobbins *Enterprise*, forewarned the merchants of Kansas City that they would be waited upon by the Hon. Thomas Jefferson, a victim of the great scourge, and at the same time a man who had lost sight of his own troubles in the awful calamity that had overtaken his fellow-citizens. It bespoke for the advocate a generous welcome and a hearty measure of aid, and presented him to the great commercial Samaritans as one of the foremost men of Kansas, the peer of the brightest and the pride of the best. The Judge thoughtfully mailed several copies of this formal introduction to the newspapers, the banks and the Board of Trade of the Southwestern metropolis. Then he brushed up his best clothes and started for the city.

A smaller man than the Judge, a man less self-contained, less conscious of the high philanthropy of his mission, less impressed with the urgency of the cause that drove him from his rural quiet into the noise and bustle of the city, would have been overwhelmed by the reflection that he was seeking the ear of strangers and the co-operation of men engrossed with their own affairs. But the Judge was not easily daunted. In less than six hours after his arrival in the city he had conversed with three reporters, and not only painted a harrowing picture of the desolating scenes along Dry Creek, but had reviewed in full the parallel circumstances of the second Punic war, and had outlined the probable policy of the Democratic party in the coming campaign. Two papers spoke of him as "one of the most distinguished of Democracy's chieftains," and a third styled him that "old wheel-horse of Democracy." The second day he was on 'Change laboring with the moneyed men, and setting forth, in his most picturesque manner, the terrors of the plague that had paralyzed the energies of Dobbins and clogged the wheels of commerce.

"Our town, gentlemen," said the Judge, "has enjoyed the closest commercial relations with your city. It is for this reason, if for no other, that we have come at once to you in our distress. I would ask, if it were feasible, that you should send a committee of your body to see for yourselves the extent of our sufferings, but time presses, and affliction brooks no delay."

Not one man in forty had ever heard of Dobbins, but the Judge was fertile in resources, and the next morning the newspapers printed diagrams of the town and Dry Creek in the very heart of an appalling waste of grasshoppers. Board of Trade men are notoriously open-handed, and this evidence of suffering touched them. Before the week was out a purse of nearly $1,500 had been presented to the Judge, and a carload of corn-meal was ordered shipped to Dobbins without delay.

Publius Scipio, returning from the second Punic war, could not have experienced a greater measure of personal satisfaction than was felt by the Judge as he took the train for Dobbins. And he argued forcibly with himself as he bowled along: "It is a principle promulgated by a great statesman that to the victors belong the spoils! Such principles, however, should be governed by circumstances. I will apply only $200 to my own expenses out of the $1,450 I have raised by my eloquence and efforts."

An hour later he said: "It would appear that I am robbing myself. I will take $100 more for my just dues."

Still a third time the devil tempted him, and he communed: "Why conceal from myself the knowledge of my necessities? Four hundred dollars will be a poor reward for my labors." And then, with the keen appreciation of a man who enjoys a quiet joke, he asked the conductor to lose no time, as every hour deprived a suffering community of means of relief.

The return of the Judge to Dobbins was welcomed by a joyous outpouring of "sufferers." The train that bore the distinguished representative of smitten agriculture brought also, from Topeka, a relief committee and a carload of donations, principally in the way of wearing-apparel, warranted grasshopper-proof. As the Judge stepped on the platform he was met by Jim Hodgman, who propounded a few blithe questions touching the present relative condition of the Punic war and the Dry Creek invasion. To these ribald taunts the Judge replied with dignity, and an adjournment was taken to 2 P. M. to allow the committee to lay out the clothing.

It must be admitted that gratitude was not one of the shining virtues of the Dobbins sufferers. As the relief committee cordially invited the victims to step up and inspect the coats and trousers generously provided for their necessities, many were the exclamations of disappointment.

"This here coat is five years old if it's a day," said Bill Nixon.

"Ain't there no watch-pocket in them trousers, Bill?" asked Sim Mayfield.

"What do you want of a watch-pocket?" said Hodgman. "Next thing you'll be wanting a watch."

"Got any white vests?" inquired Joe Morgan. Joe was the dude sufferer.

"What do we want with these old duds, anyhow?" exclaimed John Tully, with indignation. "The corn's all gone, and there ain't no need of scarecrows."

"There's a reasonable amount of sufferin' round here," said Bill, "but I'm inclined to think, from the looks of these offerin's, that the calamity has been exaggerated."

Mr. William Ray, the tenor of the Methodist choir, stepped up briskly. "There's to be an entertainment at the church to-night for the benefit of the sufferers," said he. "If no gentleman has any objections, we'll take these things to help out the costumes."

"Take 'em along, Bill," replied Joe; "they may come in handy after all."

Mr. Morgan's prediction was verified. The costumes were the glittering feature of the entertainment, and the sufferers who came early, paid their twenty-five cents each, and occupied the front seats, applauded liberally.

"It's a darned good show," said John Tully, approvingly, "and we ought to get some money out of it. But I don't see what we'd have done without them fixin's."

Judge Jefferson appeared on the stage and was greeted with a great round of applause. He unbuttoned his vest and waved his hand with dignity.

"Fellow-sufferers,— I think I may say as much, for we are all sufferers in this common cause,— I have been requested to thank our fellow-citizens for getting up this delightful entertainment for our benefit, and also to include the relief committee from Topeka that has assisted so materially in our pleasure this evening. And so I pass to another agreeable surprise. I have the pleasure of informing you that I have returned from Kansas City with a cash contribution of $1,050. I have ventured to withhold the modest sum of $50 for my expenses, and will now turn over the balance of $1,000 to your chairman."

Tremendous enthusiasm followed this announcement. Three cheers were given for the Judge, who was surrounded by his fellow-citizens and complimented for his industry and generosity. Then Jim Hodgman took the stand.

"If the meeting is agreeable," said Jim, "I should like to ask permission of the visiting committee to use their cars for the purpose of shipping our wheat."

The committee, somewhat dazed by the turn of events, thought the matter could be arranged, and the company dispersed with many bright anticipations for the future.

Three or four days after the distribution, Judge

Jefferson, Bill Nixon and two or three more of the boys were sitting in Sam Turner's grocery, when the Judge said:

"Boys, there's a load of corn-meal down on the side-track which nobody seems to claim. I'll play you a game of seven-up to see who gets it."

"I'll go you," said Bill.

So the cards were dealt and the game progressed until everybody had been frozen out save Bill and the Judge. It was the last hand. Bill lacked one point, the Judge two.

"I stand right now," said Bill; "what yer got, Jedge?"

"King high here."

"King is good. I stand on tray for low."

"Deuce here," replied the Judge.

"Darn such luck!" said Bill; "take the cornmeal, Jedge."

The Judge went out whistling a merry tune. As he passed down the street he encountered the Rev. Mr. Henry.

"Good morning, Judge," quoth the dominie.

"Howdy," replied the Judge.

"Ah, Judge," said the reverend gentleman, earnestly, "I think that Dobbins has much to be thankful for, that through the blessing of Providence it has been enabled to surmount its affliction and distress. I trust that we all appreciate the goodness and loving kindness of the Lord,"

The Judge hastily thrust a stray card into his pocket, patted his old wallet affectionately, rolled over his quid with an easy movement of his tongue, and replied, solemnly:

"He doeth all things well."

That Awful Miss Boulder.

THAT AWFUL MISS BOULDER.

Female society was all agog. At the luncheons, the teas, the little dinner-parties; at the meetings of the literary clubs; in short, wherever the ladies for pleasure or instruction came together, the first eager questions were: "Well, have you seen her?" "And pray what is she like?"

The unhappy masculine creature who is plumped down in a coterie of women at one of those times when they are supposed to be enjoying themselves may well believe that the world is given over to small things. He may deprecate, he may shrug his shoulders, he may protest in his puny lordly way, but, Heaven defend him, he is of no more consequence than my lady's cat, and much less an object of interest than my lady's poodle. Perhaps this is why the sensible man avoids afternoon gatherings when the dog-star rages.

The cause of the present social agitation was in the nature of a remarkable invasion involving delicate treatment and the most diplomatic measures. The first explosion had taken place a month before when the omniscient Mrs. Andrain, swollen with pride and information, and triumphant in the blessedness of a piece of gossip, had announced that "the Boulders are coming back." And this intelligence naturally prompted the younger generation to ask: "Who are the Boulders?"

Major Boulder had lived in Missouri at a time when "living" for a Union man was measurably precarious and never of unalloyed pleasure. Where he came from nobody seemed to know. Connecticut, said some; Ohio, others; others, New York. All agreed that he was a Yankee in the loathsome significance of the word, and the Major would not even take the trouble to deny it. If questioned sharply, he would reply that he was a lawyer, and would point to his shingle as corroborative evidence, thereby intimating that professional confidence must be remunerated. For, albeit a Yankee, it was reluctantly admitted that he was a smart Yankee. Hence the feeling against him was intensified to a virulent degree.

When South Carolina committed the indiscretion of firing on Fort Sumter, Boulder — he wasn't a major then — unreservedly declared that it was a "damned outrage," and when the State began to divide in sentiment he was among the first to join the Federal ranks. His military career was brief, for in less than nine months he came back with a desperate wound. Experience, however, didn't change his sentiments or lessen the vigor of his expressions, and so violent were his speeches that the gentlemanly and efficient contemporaneous regulator, Bill Anderson, marked him for destruction. One day the Major was missing. No great attention would have been paid to this, but, unhappily, pretty Susie Gentry was missing also. Inquiry was made at the Gentry residence. "The repo't," said the Colonel, "is cor-rect. But—

> 'have a quick eye to see;
> She hath deceived her father and may thee.'"

The Colonel was a man of wide reading and quick and pertinent phrase.

To make an otherwise unnecessary introduction desirably short, let it be remembered that the Major fled with his young bride to Colorado, speculated in mines, made a handsome fortune, and, after twenty years of good luck and happiness, yielded to the thin air, and died. His wife, now possessed of three daughters and a comfortable income, found her heart turning back to Missouri and her childhood associations. Behold them, then, fairly domesticated in the lower breathing-levels as this tale opens.

The apparently innocent question, "Have you seen her?" did not refer directly to the pretty girl who had run away with the Yankee twenty-five years before. It was prompted by the revelations of the grocer's boy, who, being on oath, testified to old Mrs. Dallas that, while delivering an order at the back door, he had seen a mannish-looking girl at the dining-room window, with a cigarette in her mouth and her feet on a dead-level with her head. This startling report Mrs. Dallas promptly communicated to Mrs. Mercer, who in turn repeated it to Mrs. Lawrence, from whom Mrs. Crawford received it, and so on until the entire community of men, women and children knew that the Boulders smoked and sat with their feet on the mantel.

"I can readily believe that story," said Mrs. Andrain, "for when my sister, Mrs. Brown, was in Paris last summer she met the eldest Miss Boulder at one of those horrid French shows where there is very little dressing and a good deal of kicking. The interest that girl took in the sight actually made my sister shudder. At last she went up to her and said: 'Why, my dear Miss Boulder, pray what are you doing here?' And the girl turned around as cool as you please and replied: 'Pray, my dear Mrs. Brown, what are *you* doing here?' My sister was a good deal surprised, but she said, very gently: 'Why, you know I'm married.' And this girl just laughed and tossed her head and answered: 'Well, by the grace of God, I hope to be.' Did you ever in your life?"

And all the ladies present agreed that they never did, and that she must be "perfectly horrid," and some remembered that she looked "healthy enough," and might be reasonably pretty were it not for a "rather cold eye" and a "bad nose." As for her dressing, it was respectable, considering that she had "come from the West."

This phrase, "from the West," is purely relative, after all. The New England man regards Buffalo as the confines of the setting sun. The Ohio man goes "West" to Illinois. In Chicago they think of the country beyond the Missouri River. Kansas remembers that it is the geographical center of the United States. In the Rocky Mountains they remind you that they are 1,200 miles east of the Pacific Ocean, and when the traveler reaches San Francisco and swears that at last he has run down the West, lo! he finds a kingdom in itself. So the pursuit is hopeless. There is no West.

Miss Boulder was not unconscious of the sensation she had created. Indeed, she rather enjoyed it. "Excuse me," she said, apologetically, to Mrs. Audrain, "if I appear to be a tenderfoot to your conventionalities." "And what," said the bewildered lady, in narrating the incident to her friends, "is a tenderfoot?"

But if to the ladies she was a revelation, to the men she was a "stunner," a "corker," a "thoroughbred," anything that in the masculine vernacular signifies a high-stepping girl out of the ordinary. She knew the latest and the best jokes, and some of them were club jokes at that. She told a story capitally, and when she laughed she gave a hearty, ringing laugh that made society shiver. In the ball-room she held court in a corner, and a very full court it was. The women turned up their noses and sniffed contemptuously at "that girl" with her "brazen manners" and her "off-color stories," but every male creature dropped around at least twice in an evening to get a bit of Rocky Mountain breeze and, perhaps with a little malicious incentive, to shock the austere proprieties of Madam Grundy.

At the dinner-table she always remembered that she had heard such a good story that wouldn't keep. And to do her justice, it was a story that had the evidences of having been kept a little too long. The ladies shivered and turned pale and red by turns, and fled precipitately at the first opportunity. All of which was highly diverting to the awful Miss Boulder, who followed the gentlemen into their smoking-retreat and said: "Now, fellows, the girls are away; let's enjoy ourselves." And the laughter and hilarity that floated back into the drawing-room made the mothers of marriageable daughters tremble with indignation and send in for their sons on the most trivial pretexts.

The catch of the season beyond peradventure was Willie Worth. Willie was the remaining prop of an illustrious house that had exercised good judgment during a wild period of real estate speculation. Timely and advantageous deaths in his family had left him with a great fortune, no positive habits of evil, and a weak and tremulous inclination to do good. Willie was tall and slender, a partial victim to inanition, too weak to work if he had the desire, and too rich if he hadn't. So he passed his time in a hopeless endeavor to spend his income and to avoid the snares of match-making mothers and the pitfalls of shrewd and calculating daughters.

The advent of the awful Miss Boulder jarred Willie from a spell of despondency. Her strong, robust figure appealed to his enfeebled sensibilities; her high animal spirits fascinated him. Her laugh went through him like the shock of an electric battery, and her stories, while they made his teeth chatter and his hair rise gently, filled him with an indescribable longing for more. At first he was content to hang on the outskirts of her admirers, but little by little he drew nearer, until one evening she asked him, kindly, why he never invited her to dance. That completed the spell, for Willie's dancing amounted to a positive disease, from which the girls shrank as they would from a plague. So Willie haunted her with his long, trembling figure and melancholy face. He even smoked a few cigarettes in order that he might be near her after dinner and catch some of the ozone which she distributed so lavishly. Perceiving which, the mothers trembled more violently and wished the more heartily that the "creature" had never left her mountain fastnesses.

In turn, Miss Boulder was attracted by the gentle Willie. It was the kindly law of opposites. She was so vigorous, so straight, so full of rich arterial blood; he so frail, so willowy, so bloodless. So she petted him, and smiled on him, and allowed him to wait on her. And one night in company she called him "Billy," a favor which he repaid with a look of the most eloquent gratitude. But beyond this matters did not progress. She had no time for sentiment.

It was at the third and final summer reception of the Prairie Club. Miss Boulder had been in unusual spirits, and her jests and sallies had paled the electric lights. Very handsome Miss Boulder looked, and in marked contrast was her perfect physical womanhood to the emaciated form of Willie, who was trembling perceptibly with weakness and pleasure. Miss Boulder was taking one of a series of ices with Willie in a corner of the summer-garden, and a pleasant hush had fallen upon the inviting scene.

"Billy," said the awful Miss Boulder, suddenly, "why don't you come down to see my kid?"

"Your wh— what?" gasped Willie.

"My kid, my baby. Don't you know that I have a baby?"

Willie wiped the cold perspiration from his

brow. "I didn't know — that is, I hadn't heard — you'll pardon me, but I don't believe I exactly understood."

Miss Boulder gave one of her invigorating laughs. "Don't say anything about it, Billy boy, for you might get me into trouble and summarily ruin my reputation. Come down to-morrow afternoon, and I'll let you into a secret."

Willie sat up late that night and smoked a cigarette, as was his custom when he was very stern and desperate. Plainly he had allowed matters to go too far. He had permitted himself to think even tenderly of a young woman who not only defied cherished conventions, but openly flaunted her improprieties in the face of her warmest and stanchest friend. It was not too late. He would show this brazen creature that he was a man *sans* — *sans* — *sans* something; he couldn't remember exactly what it was. Willie was not strong in the modern languages. And he went to bed very white from the double effect of emotion and cigarette.

But in the morning the old feeling came back. After all, it might be a mistake. Was it not an undisputed fact that this girl was a madcap to whom nothing was too sacred for a jest? Of course it was a jest. Any fool could see that, and Willie was prepared to admit in defense of his lady-love that he was very much of a fool.

So, after luncheon, having braced himself with such stimulating influence as a soda cocktail affords, Willie went down to the Boulder residence. For a moment he stood on the porch and admired the clematis that climbed up and around the column, and he recalled, with a sudden gush of feeling, that Miss Boulder had worn a dress of that color at a lawn *fête.* The reminiscence nearly took him off his feet, but he steadied himself and rang the bell. Miss Boulder answered the summons. It was shockingly unconventional, but Willie rather liked it. It made him feel that the young woman was anxious to see him, and in this event any lapse was excusable. There was a serious look in Miss Boulder's gray eyes, and almost a sadness in her voice as she said, gently:

"I was afraid that perhaps you would not come. Step in, Mr. Worth. It is cooler in the house."

Willie was greatly troubled. He had nerved himself to be calm, collected; to exhibit a frigidity bordering even upon hauteur. Had she called him Billy he was prepared to stiffen and greet her with a chilling and commonplace phrase. But "Mr. Worth" was entirely too unexpected for his programme. It brought before him a gaping abyss. On the other side of a yawning chasm stood Miss Boulder. He gazed at her helplessly and shambled into the house, his old weakness returning with alarming rapidity.

Miss Boulder preserved her gravity of tone. "You seemed so unlike yourself when we parted last night; you were so preoccupied and so silent that I was sure I had offended you. And you know, Willie" (this with a most engaging air), "that I could not bear to have you angry with me."

The young man fidgeted nervously in his chair. "I presume I was thinking of that baby."

Miss Boulder's face lighted up, and she laughed quietly. "I promised I would let you into a secret. Wait a minute, and I will produce the important element."

When she had gone to execute the writ of *habeas corpus*, Willie played with his watch-chain and endeavored to bring his shattered intellect to a proper realization of the situation. He had not untangled his wits when Miss Boulder returned with a triumphant flush on her cheeks and a great mass of seemingly superfluous clothing in her arms.

"There," said Miss Boulder, "what do you think of my little beauty?"

Willie rose irresolutely and poked feebly at the bundle with his stick. Then he drew a little nearer and clucked once or twice. Feeling the necessity of saying something, he remarked: "It's a beautiful child, but it seems to have a lot of color. Why, it's got its eyes open."

"Of course," answered Miss Boulder, with some asperity; "you don't suppose that babies are like cats, do you?"

"I didn't know," said Willie, doubtfully; "I thought perhaps some of them might be."

"Not until they're grown up," said Miss Boulder, reflectively. And she cast a wicked look across the street, where old Mrs. Dallas had her habitation.

A long silence followed. Then Willie plunged in desperately: "It doesn't look a bit like you."

"Sir!" said Miss Boulder.

"I suppose it takes after its father. I have heard somewhere that girl babies always do take after the father, though I don't see why they should. I presume it has something to do with physiology."

"On the contrary," said Miss Boulder, coolly, "the baby is the perfect picture of the mother."

Willie stared at the young girl and marveled at her extraordinary self-possession. So innocent and fair she looked, so seemingly unconscious of the great shadow she had thrown on her life. He shut his eyes and groaned inwardly.

"And now," said Miss Boulder, gayly, "now for the secret. You know, perhaps, that I do a little slumming in a quiet and private way, just for my own amusement. Doubtless, you read in the paper of the man who was killed by the falling of the elevator, and of the death of his wife from the shock two days later. It was my luck or chance to drop in at the house, and there I found this little baby. It looked so lonesome and so helpless that — well, I brought it home; and now that I have it, I suppose the whole town will be pulling me over the coals." And the awful Miss Boulder looked positively distressed.

Willie had well-nigh collapsed during the recital. He shook his feeble legs together and walked to the window. When he turned around, his face was beaming.

"Margaret — that is to say, Miss Boulder, I think I should like to hold it."

"Take care," said Miss Boulder, anxiously. "What are you feeling down there for? Don't you know that babies aren't measured by the length of their clothes? You're hunching her dress up around her neck."

"It's a beautiful baby," cried the radiant Willie, "even if it is a little too red and fat." Then, as if an inspiration had seized him: "Margaret, you come over on the sofa and hold it. I feel as if I might drop it."

So Miss Boulder sat down on the sofa and chirped to the baby and talked "goo" talk. And the infant clutched at Willie's mustache, which set that young gentleman off in a spasm of admiration. And Miss Boulder danced the baby in her arms and kissed her, and Willie leaned over and pressed his lips as near the same place as possible, and the merry minutes flew by very rapidly to all concerned. At last, in a lull of osculation, Willie straightened his long, thin legs and said, in a strained voice:

"Margaret, I have been wanting to say something to you for a long time."

"Yes, I know," replied Miss Boulder, without a particle of trepidation; "you want to ask me to marry you."

"What a girl you are!" exclaimed Willie, admiringly. "You ought to have been a mind-reader."

"Now listen, Willie," said Miss Boulder, earnestly; "I suppose if I were like most girls I should blush and simper and say, 'Oh, Mr. Worth, this is so sudden.' It's a foolish way that most girls have. They are trying to deceive you. They can tell to the minute when a man is in love with them. I have known for weeks that you cared for me, and I might have drawn you out two months ago. But I wanted to give you time to know your own mind thoroughly."

"Then you do love me," said the fluttering Willie.

"Not so fast, please. I will confess that at first I took a little malicious pleasure in getting you away from the other girls. It was such fun; they were so awfully jealous. All the old match-makers in town were after you, and how they glared when I

whirled you up past their corner. And I did it
pretty often. But after a while I learned to miss
you when you didn't come around, and to look for
you. You were always so nice and gentle and
thoughtful and kind — and — and "—— Here the
awful Miss Boulder fell to kissing the baby raptur-
ously.

"Then," said Willie, decidedly, "I don't see why
we shouldn't get married right off."

"There's something yet," went on Miss Boulder,
slowly. "I'm an unconventional girl, and I know
I make awful breaks. I was brought up in the
West, where I did as I pleased, and cared for nobody's opinion. I can't say that I care very much
now, but I'm not going to marry any man who is
ashamed of me."

"I'm unconventional myself," said Willie,
eagerly. "I hate these forms and ceremonies, this
solemn sitting in state until a maid comes in and
breaks the deadly stillness by whispering that dinner is served. I like a house where they ring the
dinner-bell, and people just sort of drop down and
eat."

"But you wouldn't like," said Miss Boulder,
smilingly, "a wife who has the reputation of being
loud, of telling 'men-stories,' and" (bitterly) "of
smoking cigarettes and cocking her feet on the
mantel like a man."

"I must admit," said the truthful Willie, "that

some of your stories are pretty tough, but after we are married you might work 'em off on me in private and let me pass on 'em. As for these people here, what do we care for them? I've got lots of money, and, if things don't go right, the country is big, and Europe isn't shut up yet."

Miss Boulder did not reply. She toyed with the baby's chubby hand a moment. Then she looked up suddenly, and tears were in her eyes.

Willie was deeply affected. "Don't cry, Margaret," he said, hastily; "you're too strong and too sort of manly to cry. I think it would be better to let me do all the crying."

The girl smiled and said gently: "Come, Willie, run away now, there's a good boy. We both need a little time to think." Then she added, naïvely: "You might come around this evening after the baby has gone to bed."

Willie, who had acquired marvelous strength in his legs, and whose face radiated all the happiness of his feelings, moved briskly to the door. A thought struck him, and he returned. The awful Miss Boulder stood in the middle of the room, holding the baby in her arms, kissing it and cooing to it as it laughed in her face. And Willie thought he saw in her expression a loveliness, a gentleness he had never seen before. The girl looked up and blushed. Willie took a step forward and said, awkwardly:

"Margaret, I thought I would like — that is, if you don't object — er-r — won't you let me kiss the baby again?"

"Oh, Willie!"

"Oh, Margaret!"

The Luck of Silas Scott.

THE LUCK OF SILAS SCOTT.

TRAGEDY should be short. Tales of sorrow and despair must be quickly told. There is so much that is bright and beautiful and alluring in life that he is abnormally constituted who would linger and grieve over the dark places in human existence. It is right that the reader should know in advance a little of the misery that is awaiting him. If he cannot be forewarned in the actual events of life it does not follow that the same rule must apply to his literature. He deserves a measure of consideration from his story-teller, a sort of sign-board that may act as a danger-signal. This is a tale with a deep coating of umber, and he who reads may run, if the paraphrase is permitted. At all events, he cannot say that the warning has not been frank and timely.

Far out in Western Kansas stretches a vast country, a veritable empire, rising gradually to the Rocky Mountains, a country to tax human patience, human industry, human ingenuity. It is a country that might have exhausted the possibilities of an Arabian night with its capriciousness, its kaleidoscopic changes, its splendors, when fickle

Nature is favorable; its terrors, when she frowns. It is a country of which the Government says to the long caravan of immigration: "Why delay in the poor, sterile land of small things when all this may be had for the mere asking?" So the tide ebbs and flows; they go and come, and they come and go, and the great drama of life, with its shifts and changes, is acted over and over in the countless stories of the wide-stretching plains.

The voyager adrift in a rowboat on the Atlantic has no greater, no more crushing sense of his utter loneliness than the traveler who finds himself alone on the plains of the West. One is land, the other water; otherwise the conditions are the same. The sun rises at the dead level of the horizon and goes down in the same terrible expanse. In the summer it brings its seemingly endless hours of heat and torment; in the winter it only mocks at misery and fear. To add to the perplexity of the traveler on the plains, Nature herself conspires to taunt him. Now he sees a beautiful grove with its restful shade and running stream, and quickly it vanishes in the cruel disappointment of the mirage. And now almost at his hand he welcomes a landmark or a haven of refuge, and presses eagerly forward, mile after mile, only to see it dancing on before him, deluding him with the magnifying properties of the atmosphere. If the summer has been dry, as the summer usually is, the earth is brown and baked, the streams are gone, and miles of cheerless sand are the only promise of the day passing and the days to come. Such pictures as these, and common as they are, the traveler cannot exaggerate.

Silas Scott was a farmer in one of the Eastern States, a plain, plodding, hard-working man with enough education to keep abreast of the times, and enough ambition to desire to better his lot. Silas lived in a moving neighborhood. One by one his friends and acquaintances dropped out, and word came back to Silas that they had all gone West and prospered. So Silas in time, for he was a slow thinker, felt the Western fever in his blood. He was making a living for himself and family, but it was a living that came hard and slowly, and there he was, tilling a few acres of ground to call his own, when the Government was knocking at his door, reproaching him for his conservatism, and asking him why he didn't go out and take 160 acres of land in the West, just for the claiming. Silas thought it out in his ponderous way, and the temptation was too strong. He was young, his wife was young, his children were strong and healthy; the opportunity was dazzling. So into far Kansas came Silas with his family and began a new existence on the plains.

The story of Silas Scott in his pursuit of an easy living is the story that has been told a thousand times by those who believe in the hard and doubtful qualities of luck. It was bad luck that led Silas to the selection of his quarter section remote from those who might have been kind and helpful neighbors, and in a spot where only the most favorable conditions of weather could assure a profitable crop. It was bad luck that the year was one of the most disastrous ever known to the farmers of Kansas; that the burning sun and the unbroken drought began the work of destruction which the fierce, hot winds speedily completed. But Silas was a man of character, with a good deal of dogged determination. He had gone to work to put up his little adobe house — not as comfortable as the one he had left, the little frame dwelling back East, but good enough for a start, and promising to lead to better things. He worked early and late, studied the conditions of the soil, and made all the calculations and allowances that a careful man should make. There was no time for pleasure or relaxation, and there was no thought of it. What mattered one or two years of toil if they led to a peaceful future and an abundancy of fortune? So Silas and his wife worked on uncomplainingly, and if the wife grew a little thinner, and both were careworn and more weary as the weeks passed by, neither had time to notice it.

"It'll be all right, Nancy," said Silas, when the spring storms came on with irresistible force and washed away the results of his early labors; "luck is against us at the start, but it will turn."

"It's all right, Nancy," he repeated at the end of the first year, when he sat down to figure up his season's profits and found himself far behind his original calculations. "A bad beginning makes a good ending."

And when, in the second summer, the long dry spell set in, and the grain blistered and cracked in the burning sun, his pluck never forsook him, and his "It's all right," was as firm as ever. Then the winds came hot and furious, and the earth seemed on fire; the creeks dried up, and vegetation perished. "It's all right," he muttered, less hopefully.

"Don't cry, Nancy," he said, when the baby, born in that atmosphere of despair, gave up the struggle and yielded its little life. "Perhaps it's for the best. It's all right, or it wouldn't have come about." And his own voice quivered.

But the mother, sitting by the bed and closing the baby's eyes, said not a word. She was back again in the old home, where the trees were green and the brooks were full. The pain in her heart was stilled, for memory had carried her away to happier times and deluded her with a dream of the past.

All that suffocating day Silas sat under the shadow of the shed, fashioning the rude coffin for the dead child. The hot winds were still blowing with that peculiar, menacing hiss that came as the breath of the venomous serpent, but Silas worked on, struggling with his rising doubts, and vainly endeavoring to solace himself with his favorite maxim, "It's all right." In the house the mother was preparing for the burial, which was to take place when the sun went down. On the baby's breast and in his tiny hand she had placed little bunches of dried flowers, the only offering that Nature could give, and from the trunk she had taken a battered prayer-book, that Silas might read the service for the dead and give her baby at least the semblance of a Christian burial.

In the evening, as they stood around the little grave, the father, the mother and the elder children, hushed and awed in the first manifestation of irremediable affliction, Silas, in his dull, heavy way, stumbled through the service his wife had marked:

"I am the resurrection and the life. . . . I know that my Redeemer liveth. . . . And now, Lord, what is my hope? . . . He heapeth up riches and cannot tell who shall gather them. . . . We brought nothing into this world, and it is certain we can carry nothing out."

These and many similar passages Silas read and did not understand, for he was a dull man, and grasped only the tangible things of the present.

He filled in the grave and followed his wife into the house, while the children played about in the joyless way that characterized their lives.

That night, while the children were sleeping and Silas sat in his chair pondering over the shaping of events, Nancy stood in the doorway and looked out across the plains. The moon was full and bright, but to the woman it was not the same kindly moon that her girlhood remembered. Far away came the wail of the coyote, and Nancy shuddered. She had heard that half-human, querulous cry a thousand times, but never before had it come to her with such significance. She shut the door hastily, drew close to her husband, and sat down beside him. Then she put her hand on his arm and said, gently:

"Silas, why not give up? We've done all that human beings can do, and we're as far away as ever. What good can come from fighting fate?"

Silas moved a little uneasily. "Why, it's all right, Nancy," he said, soothingly.

"That's what you've always said," exclaimed the woman, with sudden energy. "It has been 'all right' with you when our hearts and our common sense told us it was all wrong. Perhaps our baby thought it was all right when he came to brighten us up a bit. It is all right with him now, and it will be all right with us when we go to join him."

"I wouldn't talk that way, Nancy," said the man, slowly.

"How else can I talk?" replied the wife. "We have lived this wretched life without a spark of hope, a particle of encouragement. Bad luck has followed us from the start and has shown us no future. We are alone, without friends and without comfort. Every morning the sun comes up like a ball of fire and brings fresh misery to this desert. You know what that awful sun means, Silas. Look in the insane asylum of this State and find its victims. What has become of old Prouty, a stronger man than you, Silas, who defied its power? A month ago he was carried away a hopeless maniac, and we have remained to invite his fate. Every night I go to bed thinking of old Prouty and listening to the mocking of the wind and the howling of the wolf. I can't stand it any longer."

"I've tried to be as easy on you as I can," said the man, by way of blundering apology.

"I don't find fault with you, Silas, but I'm hungry for the old home. We were happy there if we were poor. We worked hard, but we always made a living, and if we got a little tired and despondent at times we had our friends, and the little farm with the great green shade-trees, and the birds singing in them. Here we have nothing but a huge plain and a blazing sun. Let's go back,

Silas, where at least we can find a little happiness, and — where there is a God."

The woman put her head on her husband's shoulder. Then she said, a little more calmly: "Did you believe the words you repeated at our baby's grave? Did you really think there was a God in this horrible place to hear them? 'I am the resurrection and the life.' Can a God bring comfort to those who mock him by calling to him from a desert where their foolish ambitions have led them? Why should we try to heap up riches or carry to the grave more than we brought into the world?"

Silas looked bewildered. The woman's swift application of the texts began to penetrate his dull reason. He stared helplessly at his wife, and patted her on the shoulder for an answer.

"I don't complain for myself, Silas. I don't care much what becomes of me, except at times when the old home feeling comes back. But I see you growing ten years older in a single summer. I see the anxious look and the furrows in your face. I know you're unhappy and losing heart. And I see our children growing up neglected and ignorant. We had opportunities and a fair chance when we were young. Oh, Silas, let's go back, if only for their sakes."

The woman broke down. The man, too, felt himself strangely stirred. He got up and walked to the door. One glance was enough to show him the ruin of the summer and the hopelessness of the year. He thought in his turn of the little home back yonder, and of the pleasant times they had on the small profits of their industry. There was the little red school-house — the same one he went to when he was a boy. And the old meeting-house too. He found himself wondering whether they had put on that fresh coat of paint they were discussing when he came away. And the lane that led down to the squire's. And the old apple-tree that stood right at the left of the bend. And Bill Simpson's fishing-hole. And Thompson's grocery, where the boys elected a President of the United States every Saturday night. Silas felt his eyes getting moist.

On the other hand, what would the boys say if he gave up beaten and went back? Ought he to surrender to a little momentary weakness? Jim Higgins had gone away and succeeded, and so had Henry Cole, and so had John Grubb, the most shiftless man in the county. Could he go back and acknowledge that he had been taken in? Could he stand up and hear old Bill Simpson say: "Waal, here's Si hum ag'in; jest as I perdicted, by gum"?

Silas took a turn around the house and paused at the baby's grave. "It wasn't much of a fight he made," he muttered. "I guess that's the way with all children." And a horrible fear took hold of him all at once, as he thought of the little ones huddled asleep in a corner of the miserable room. So he came back, and, going up to the bed, gazed long and intently upon them, then turned to his wife, sitting patient and silent where he had left her. And he looked into her wan face, and the flush came into his own. Stooping down, he kissed the tired eyes and said, as if a great load had been lifted from his heart:

"It's all right, Nancy. It's all right, mother. Good luck has come at last. We're going back."

www.ingramcontent.com/pod-product-compliance
Lightning Source LLC
Chambersburg PA
CBHW020803230426
43666CB00007B/832